Getting into Canada

Getting into Canada

How to make a successful application for permanent or temporary residence

BENJAMIN KRANC
AND
ELENA CONSTANTIN

howtobooks

To my wife, Tina – BK

To the readers of this book; may it encourage you
to pursue your dream of coming to Canada – EC

Published by How To Books Ltd,
3 Newtec Place, Magdalen Road,
Oxford OX4 1RE, United Kingdom.
Tel: (01865) 793806. Fax: (01865) 248780.
email: info@howtobooks.co.uk
http://www.howtobooks.co.uk

First edition 2004

British Library Cataloguing in Publication Data.
A catalogue record for this book is available from
the British Library.

Produced for How To Books by Deer Park Productions, Tavistock
Typeset by Kestrel Data, Exeter, Devon
Cover design by Baseline Arts Ltd, Oxford
Printed and bound by Cromwell Press Ltd, Trowbridge, Wiltshire

NOTE: The material contained in this book is set out in good
faith for general guidance and no liability can be accepted
for loss or expense incurred as a result of relying in particular
circumstances on statements made in the book. Laws and
regulations are complex and liable to change, and readers should
check the current position with the relevant authorities before
making personal arrangements.

Contents

PERMANENT RESIDENCE CATEGORIES

Preface

Canada continues to be front and centre as a destination for many people around the world. Some want to come for a short time, some want to come forever. All need to understand the issues involved in getting here.

The ever-changing dynamics of world issues, including economic, labour movement, security, and other issues have created a situation whereby Canada has needed to modify its immigration system. Indeed, the situation is such that the immigration system is in a state of constant modification and re-modification. The rate of change is extremely high, and people who are not careful about keeping up-to-date with the changes, may be surprised to find the gates closed to them. Conversely, strong knowledge of the system will open doors and offer opportunities that people may not have realized are available. Industry sector initiatives, provincial nominee programs, various pilot projects, all offer opportunities that may permit someone to get to Canada in a timely and effective manner.

We hope that this book highlights the opportunities, and restrictive issues, that face prospective visitors, workers, students, and immigrants, so that you may be aware of the possibilities, and be wary of the pitfalls. The book has been expanded from its previous format that covered only permanent residence issues, to now include discussion of various programs and initiatives that you can put to use. It also expands on the issues within permanent residence, and elaborates on some of the restrictive issues of which readers must be wary. Though it is no substitute for proper legal advice, we hope that readers will gain an understanding of the Canadian immigration system, as they begin their journey to Canada.

Benjamin A. Kranc and Elena Constantin
Toronto

1

Getting Started

1:1 INTRODUCTION AND OVERVIEW OF IMMIGRATION PROGRAMS

So you are somewhere around the world and are thinking that perhaps you would like to come to Canada. We wish to give you the opportunity to become familiar with the options available to you. We hope that *Getting into Canada* will help you understand the process and thus assist you in finding your way easily through the process, so that you can soon be *en route* to Canada.

You may wish to permanently establish yourself in Canada. In that case, you would have to apply for permanent resident status. The immigration programs under which you can obtain permanent residence are the following:

♦ skilled worker;

♦ family category (sponsored by a family member who is a Canadian citizen or permanent resident);

♦ business category, and;

♦ provincial nominee programs.

Applying to come to Canada as a student or as a worker, or simply as a visitor, would give you, if your application were approved, the right to temporary residence in Canada.

Each of the seven immigration programs mentioned above is discussed in more detail in the chapters that follow. The figures in each chapter and the schedules at the conclusion of the book provide you with additional information and samples of documents/forms that are relevant to particular applications.

Getting into Canada also provides you with other tools useful in understanding what lies ahead of you. These tools include a glossary with definitions of terms commonly used in the Canadian immigration field and in this book, and internet addresses that can provide you with additional information, should you wish to explore a topic in even more detail. Before we begin focusing on each of the immigration programs mentioned above, let's consider some general issues.

1:2 SOME PRACTICAL INFORMATION AND ADVICE

1:2.1 What to do first

If you are seriously considering coming to Canada, you should begin by finding out which Canadian mission abroad, be it an Embassy, High Commission or consulate,[1] you must

---

[1]If you are wondering what the difference is between an Embassy and a High Commission, it's this: Embassies are called High Commissions if they are situated in Commonwealth countries. Note that an Embassy, High Commission or consulate handling immigration matters is often referred to as a visa office or visa post. Note that a consulate is another type of 'diplomatic office', often serving as a branch to a particular Embassy.

contact in order to obtain information, application packages and additional assistance if needed.

Canada does not have a visa office in every country of the world. Many visa posts abroad are responsible for processing applications originating in a number of designated countries. To find out which visa office would process your permanent residence application,[2] see Schedule 1 on page 219.[3] When applying for permanent residence, you may apply at the visa post responsible for processing the applications from your country of citizenship or the country where you have legally resided for at least a year at the time of making your application. For temporary residence applications, you must have, or be able to have, legal status in the country where the visa post to which you are applying is situated.

1:2.2 How to get the documents that you need (the required forms and the accompanying guidelines)

The forms used by Canadian immigration authorities and the guidelines that accompany them can be obtained in three ways. One way is by contacting the relevant visa office and asking how you can pick them up or asking that they be mailed to you. The Canadian Government makes them available to everyone, free of charge.

Secondly, if you have access to the internet, you can download the forms and the guidelines (called 'Guide') online, from the Canadian Immigration Department's general web

---

[2]For the remainder of the book, we will refer to this visa office as 'the relevant visa office'.

[3]You can also visit the site of Citizenship and Immigration Canada (CIC) at **www.cic.gc.ca** for updated information on this topic.

site, at **www.cic.gc.ca**. Please note that **there is one item that you should always obtain from the relevant visa office**, either by mail or from their particular web site[4] – the checklist for the particular application that you are making. It contains the list of all the forms and supporting documents[5] that must be submitted when making a certain application. **Many visa offices have their own checklist for every type of application.** The checklists that are available on the general CIC site (some of which we have included as figures in this book) should only be used as a general reference. When it comes to making an actual application, you should obtain and rely only on the checklist from the relevant visa office.

If you wish to download the forms and guidelines online, please note that the guidelines are available in HTML format and as pdf files. The forms are only available as pdf files. A file with a 'pdf' extension can only be viewed if you have Acrobat Reader[6] software installed on your computer. If you have this software, you can either print the guidelines and blank forms online, or download the files onto your computer, and then view and/or print copies of them whenever you need to.

Thirdly, if you plan to use the services of a professional immigration service provider, you should check with them for instructions and forms.

---

[4]See Schedule 7 on p. 243 for a list of web site addresses.
[5]Examples of supporting documents are identity documents, letters of employment, bank statements, etc.
[6]You can download Acrobat Reader for free at **www.adobe.com/products/ acrobat**.

1:2.3 Filling in the forms generally

There are two ways in which you can fill in the forms.

Firstly, you can fill in the forms by hand (using a black pen) or by using a typewriter. If you are writing the information by hand, please remember to print it legibly. Certainly, by hand is the least attractive option (and attractiveness counts!).

The second option is to do it on your computer. If you have Acrobat Reader, you can type the information in the forms; however, you won't be able to save it, so you will have to complete a form in one session. To actually save the information in the forms, you would need to have installed the Adobe Acrobat software. While the forms can be downloaded online and viewed with the assistance of Acrobat Reader (which, as mentioned above, can be downloaded for free), Adobe Acrobat must be purchased.

It may be costly to buy Adobe Acrobat simply for the purpose of filling in the forms. If you have it, use it to fill in the forms and then print completed forms directly onto blank paper. If you don't own the software, you'll have to complete each form in one session, as noted above, or print the blank forms and then resort to typing or handwriting the information.

We recommend that before you start completing the forms by any method, you ensure that you have handy additional photocopies of the blank forms; you should practise filling in the various sections on photocopies first, before you fill in the final set which you intend to submit.

We also recommend that when you fill in forms, you have on your desk the applicable government guidelines (which you obtain as mentioned in section 1:2.2). Please note that each type of application that can be made is accompanied by a different set of guidelines. The guidelines will answer at least some of the questions you may have along the way; they will provide you with clarification with respect to what information needs to go into a particular section of the application. Do your best to follow the instructions provided. If you have questions, contact the relevant visa office and ask for assistance or seek professional assistance.

1:2.3.a What to avoid when filling in forms
In terms of the information you provide to the Canadian authorities, please note that it is a serious offence to give false or misleading information on your application forms. The Canadian immigration authorities may check to verify your responses, and misrepresentations, depending on your circumstances, can result in the refusal of your application, the cancellation of your visa,[7] the revocation of your citizenship, your deportation from Canada, bans from entering Canada and criminal charges being laid against you.

Apart from inaccurate information, there are additional things that you should avoid when filling in forms.

[7]If your application is accepted and information you provide on the forms changes before you arrive in Canada, you must inform, in writing, the relevant visa office. You must do this even if your visa has already been issued.

◆ **Don't leave a section blank.**

It is important to note that, when filling in the forms, you should not leave any section blank. Where there is no information you can include in a particular section (for example, where you are required to give details of military service undertaken, and you have never served in the military), instead of leaving the section blank, write 'N/A' (which stands for 'Not Applicable'). This way, the immigration official will know for sure that the section does not apply to you and will not have to wonder whether or not you forgot to fill it in. By doing so, you will eliminate from the start a potential cause of delay in the processing of your application.

◆ **Don't leave time gaps if requested to account for an entire period of time.**

Another thing that you should not do is leave time gaps in those sections that require you to account for all the time between two dates, like, for example, in a section that asks you to list all the addresses where you have resided in the past ten years.

◆ **Don't provide contradictory information and don't leave apparent contradictions unexplained.**

In your application do not provide information that is contradictory. If there are apparent contradictions, make sure you explain them in a cover letter to your application.

◆ **Do not leave sections incomplete.**

If you run out of space when filling in a particular section, attach a separate sheet of paper to the form and indicate the number of the question you are answering.

1:2.4 What to avoid when submitting an application

It is helpful to remember, at any stage of the process, that there will be a person who will be assessing your application. Make their task easier to accomplish by ensuring that the forms and documents you submit are well organised. Some suggestions include:

◆ ensure pages that should be together are stapled or paper clipped;

◆ do not bind your application or put the pages in a ring binder;

◆ do not enclose individual pages in plastic, envelopes or folders;

◆ do not tie, sew, bolt or glue the pages together;

◆ do not use multiple staples on a page;

◆ do not send multiple copies of identical documents;

◆ do not fax or e-mail your application.

You should check with the relevant visa office and ask about the accepted methods of submitting applications (e.g. general mail, in person, by courier). You should also verify with them what are the acceptable methods of payment. In addition, make sure that you print your name and address on the top left-hand side of the envelope containing your application.

1:2.4.a What factors can slow down the processing of your application?

The following factors typically delay the processing of applications:

◆ incomplete or unsigned application forms;

◆ incorrect, incomplete address or failure to notify the immigration authorities of a change of address;

◆ missing documents or fees;

◆ unclear or non-certified photocopies of documents;

◆ documents not accompanied by a certified English or French translation;

◆ insufficient postage.

In general, you should make sure that you provide the required information and supporting documents at the time you are making the application. If you submit items in stages, the processing of your application will take considerably longer (and may even result in refusal before you get to submit the further papers). You should also avoid unnecessary enquiries to the visa office once your application has been submitted.

There may be additional factors delaying the processing of the application, such as a medical condition that may require additional tests or consultation, family situations such as impending divorce, or custody or custody or maintenance issues, a criminal or security problem.

1:3 WHAT A TYPICAL APPLICATION WILL INCLUDE

Every application that you make will include the **fees**, the completed **forms** and the **supporting documents**.

The fees differ depending on the type of application made and the number of people included in the application. For a list of the fees payable at the time of the writing of these materials, see Schedule 4 (page 228). For updated information about the fees at the time you are making your application, visit the site of CIC at **www.cic.gc.ca**.

The forms to be completed can be obtained as specified in section 1:2.2. To complete them, use the guidelines provided by the Government of Canada and contact the relevant visa office overseas or CIC call centres inland[8] if you have further questions.

The supporting documents that you must include are the documents specified in the checklist from the relevant visa office, a checklist which you should make sure you obtain as highlighted above in section 1:2.2. In general, supporting documents include:

◆ valid passport/travel document;

◆ proof of means of support like bank account statements, bank drafts in convertible currency, travellers' cheques;

◆ police certificates and clearances;

◆ other documents relevant in the context of a particular application. For example, in the context of an application for a student permit, you would have to submit as

[8]See Schedule 8 (page 246) for CIC call centres information.

a supporting document the letter of admission from a Canadian educational institution.

In addition, if you are not a citizen of the country from which you are applying, you must provide proof of your current immigration status in that country.

1:4 ABOUT HIRING A REPRESENTATIVE

Much of the general information needed to make an application is made available to you by the Canadian Government.

Many people, however, hire an immigration lawyer or consultant. While faster or more favourable processing is not given to people with representatives, a good representative can be a great asset. At the same time, a poor representative may hinder you, so you should be careful in your selection.

Choosing a representative is a difficult task. Though the term 'specialist' is thrown about like a football, knowing who truly has experience may be difficult to discern. You must make sure that you do your research: check references and visit the web sites of consultant groups like **www.opic.org** and **www.aicc.ca**, or of the relevant Law Societies of Canada (for Ontario, for instance, it is the Law Society of Upper Canada, at **www.lsuc.on.ca**). Note that as of the time of preparation of these materials, the government is set to regulate consultants. Information can be found at **www.csic-scci.ca**

With this basic ammunition in hand, let us now explore the world of Canadian immigration processing, and what you need to know.

2

Practical Issues Relating to Employment in Canada

Except for students and 'tourists' the vast majority of people coming to Canada, whether for temporary or permanent purposes, hope and expect to work here.

This chapter provides you with an overview of some of the relevant aspects related to working in Canada. Throughout the book we will refer you back to this chapter, and we suggest that you become familiar with it before reading the remainder of the book.

2:1 THE NATIONAL OCCUPATIONAL CLASSIFICATION

Canada maintains a list containing all the occupations practised in the country and their descriptions. It is called the **National Occupational Classification (NOC)** list and it can be accessed online at **www23.hrdc-drhc.gc.ca**, the website of Human Resources and Skills Development Canada (HRSDC).

Professions and trades are divided into different categories on the basis of **skill level** and also on the basis of **skill type**.

This division is of particular importance depending on the type of application you may wish to make.

There are four skill level categories.

Skill level A
◆ University degree (Bachelor's, Master's or PhD).

Skill level B
◆ Two to three years of post-secondary education at community college, institute of technology, or

◆ two to four years of apprenticeship training, or

◆ three to four years of secondary school and more than two years of on-the-job training, training courses or specific work experience.

Please note that the following occupations are assigned to skill level B:

◆ occupations with supervisory responsibilities;

◆ occupations with significant health and safety responsibilities (e.g., fire fighters, police officers and registered nursing assistants).

Skill level C
◆ One to four years of secondary school education, or

◆ up to two years of on-the-job training, training courses or specific work experience.

Skill level D

◆ Up to two years of secondary school and short work demonstration or on-the-job training.

Skill type categories

There are ten skill type categories:

0 Management occupations.

1 Business, finance and administration occupations.

2 Natural and applied sciences and related occupations.

3 Health occupations.

4 Occupations in social science, education, government service and religion.

5 Occupations in art, culture, recreation and sport.

6 Sales and service occupations.

7 Trades, transport and equipment operators and related occupations.

8 Occupations unique to primary occupations.

9 Occupations unique to processing, manufacturing and utilities.

On the HRSDC site **www.23.hrdc.gc.ca** you will find, under the 2001 version of the NOC, a link called 'Occupational Descriptions' that will take you to a page listing all these ten categories. Under each category you can find a detailed list of occupations and their four-digit NOC codes. By clicking on a code, you can access the description of that particular profession or trade.

It is important to note that occupations in Canada fall within two categories: regulated and non-regulated. If you plan to come to Canada, you should find out as much as possible about the practice of your profession or trade in Canada.

2:2 REGULATED OCCUPATIONS

There are two main types of regulated occupations in Canada: regulated professions (e.g. physicians, nurses, lawyers) and apprenticeable trades (e.g. mechanics, plumbers, welders).

To legally practise in a regulated occupation, you must obtain a licence or certification from a professional or regulatory body, or be registered with that body. To be able to do so, you will have to meet the qualification requirements established by the regulatory body. These requirements may differ from one province or territory to another. It is important to note also that some occupations may be regulated in some provinces and non-regulated in others.

To find out if a profession or trade is regulated in Canada, look at the information contained in the NOC at **www.23.hrdc.gc.ca**; the detailed description of a particular profession or trade in the NOC will provide you, under the heading of 'Employment Requirements', with information as to whether **licensing**, **certification** or **registration** with a professional body is required.

To find out if your occupation is regulated in the province or territory where you intend to settle, and to find out about the qualification requirements, visit:

◆ Work Destinations – A Guide to Work and Relocation in Canada, at **www.workdestinations.ca**
Under the 'Regulated Occupations' category, select 'Search the Regulated Occupations Database'; if you know the NOC code of the occupation of interest to you, you can do a search on the right-hand side of the screen.

If you click on the 'Search Results' link, you will find more information about the requirements applicable to your occupation in various provinces and territories.

For additional information, including contact information, visit:

◆ Canadian Apprenticeship Forum, at **www.caf-fca.org**
Under 'Links' you will find the contact information for various organisations and departments related to apprenticeship in Canada.

◆ Canadian Information Centre for International Credentials, at **www.cicic.ca**
Under the 'Information on Specific Professions and Trades' link, you may wish to review the information available under the link, 'list all occupational profiles currently available'.

◆ Work destinations – A Guide to Work and Relocation in Canada, at **www.workdestinations.ca**
Under the 'Addresses and References' category, you can find a link to Occupational Associations.

2:2.1 RECOGNITION OF QUALIFICATIONS IN REGULATED OCCUPATIONS

The recognition of credentials, training or experience acquired abroad is the responsibility of the provincial/territorial professional regulatory body. The way to have your qualifications recognised is different in each province and territory, and for each occupation. In many cases, you can only apply to have your qualifications recognised once you are in Canada.

You may be asked to:

◆ submit to a review of your foreign qualifications;

◆ take a language test;

◆ complete a professional exam;

◆ do supervised work.

The websites mentioned above can provide you with the relevant details, including the names and addresses of the organisations you may contact for further information.

You will need to research in your own field in order to find out the costs and specific requirements related to licensing, certification or registration, as well as the recommended procedure for assessment of your qualifications.

2:3 NON-REGULATED OCCUPATIONS

There are no specific requirements applicable to non-regulated occupations. About 80% of the Canadian workforce are employed in non-regulated occupations.

2:3.1 Recognition of qualifications in non-regulated occupations

In the case of non-regulated occupations, the individual employer will set the qualification requirements for a particular position. The recognition of foreign qualifications will also be at the discretion of your potential employer.

2:4 HOW TO IMPROVE YOUR CHANCES OF GETTING WORK IN CANADA

Though the legal issues will differ in permanent residence applications (where a job offer will follow the permanent residence application) versus temporary work permit applications (where an application will follow a job offer), there are some practical issues of which you should be aware.

The process of securing work in Canada involves a number of steps, including extensive research of the job market and the drafting of a good resumé and of individualised cover letters. It may also involve retaining the services of an employment agency and obtaining an assessment of educational credentials, particularly in the case of someone looking for a job from outside Canada or of someone who has completed his or her education abroad.

2:4.1 Researching the job market

Many online resources allow job-seekers around the world access to Canadian job market information. Two major websites are:

www.workopolis.ca
www.monster.ca

For additional sites posting job-related information visit:

◆ Work Destinations – A Guide to Work and Relocation in Canada:
www.workdestinations.ca
You may wish to review the information posted on the links under 'Finding Work' and 'The Labour Market'.

◆ Human Resources Development Canada:
www.hrsdc/en/home.shtml

In addition, you can find job-related information in the classifieds of the Canadian newspapers available online. You can also subscribe to periodicals such as *Canada Employment Weekly* or order various publications on the topic.

2:4.2 Writing a cover letter

Many of the websites listed above include practical advice with regard to this aspect of a job application. We would add a few suggestions. For example, if you are applying from overseas you should indicate in your cover letter when you expect to get your immigration status or your work permit if you do not have it already.

The purpose of a cover letter is to highlight aspects of your resumé as well as information about yourself that is not readily apparent. Write about specific work experience or training that is directly relevant to the job you are applying for. State why you are interested in the job and what you can bring to it and the organisation. Try to get your personality across a bit as well.

2:4.3 Writing a resumé

As with cover letters, you can find advice about writing a resumé on many of the websites listed above. We would add that you should make sure that your resumé is no more than two pages long. As a general principle, you should put your employment history first, but if your education credentials are particularly impressive, you may consider listing them first instead. Also, always list the most recent experience first within your work history and education sections.

Figures 1 and 2 show a sample cover letter and a brief resumé. With regard to the resumé, a person with more experience would continue on to a second page, or a second page could be used to list volunteer work and other work experience or extra-curricular activities. You can also add a line listing hobbies and interests.

Name
Mailing address
Telephone number
Mobile telephone number
E-mail

Date

«ContactName»
«ContactTitle»
«ContactCompany»
«ContactStreet»
«ContactCity», «ContactProvince»
«ContactPostCode», «ContactCountry»

Dear «ContactSalutation»:

Your advertisement on Monster for a (insert job title) fits my experience and qualifications perfectly, and I am writing to express my interest in and enthusiasm for the position. As an accomplished sales leader, my career achievements have included seven-figure revenue growth, international market penetration and successful product launch for leading global corporations.

In addition to my desire to join your team, you will find I am a dedicated and driven professional whose recent accomplishments include:

◆ **An increase of international sales from 1% of the company's total revenue to 75%,** capturing more than half of the entire European market and one-third of the Latin American market within two years.
◆ **Dramatic expansion of customer base,** leading to seven-figure revenue growth rates that far exceed the pace of larger, more established competitors.
◆ **Development of a 75-member dealer network** across 30 countries in six continents.
◆ **Attainment of 100% customer retention rate** through expert relationship-building skills and a commitment to a solution-focused, service-first sales approach.
◆ **Launch of a new London office,** expected to double sales revenue by 2004.
◆ **Introduction of three innovative product lines,** following comprehensive market research and competitive-intelligence gathering.

Fig. 1. Sample cover letter[1].

Your software products are truly on the cutting-edge of technology – you offer products that can change the way a company conducts business on the internet. I am excited by this technology and would be able to translate this excitement to a business benefit for your current and future clients. If you agree that my qualifications are a close fit to your needs, I would be delighted to meet with you personally to discuss strategies for expanding (name of company's) market presence.

I will follow up with you in a few days to answer any questions you may have. In the meantime, you may reach me at (phone number) or via e-mail at (e-mail address). I look forward to our conversation.

Sincerely,
Dina Smith

Fig. 1. continued.

Jill Doe

14 Blackburn Road
Suffolk JW2 46X, England
jdoe@.email.com
Tel: 44-1473-290-821
Fax: 44-1473-290-263

JOB OBJECTIVE: Financial services marketing manager

MARKETING EXPERIENCE

ATK Marketing Inc. 1995 to present
Brand manager

◆ Responsible for marketing line of CD ROMs.

[1]From **www.monster.ca**.

Nichemarketing Ltd   1993–1995
Marketing representative

◆ Promoted financial products for mutual fund client.

FINANCIAL INDUSTRY EXPERIENCE

Bowman Mutual Funds   1990–1993
Financial assistant

◆ Assisted broker in all aspects of financial services.
◆ Co-ordinated stock and asset research.

EDUCATION

Penticton School of Economics   1986–1990
BA Honours in Economics and Political Science
Dean's List 1987–1990

Lakeside Secondary   1980–1986
General Certificate of Education A Levels in maths, statistics,
economics and English

OTHER SKILLS/DETAILS

◆ Member of the Financial Planners Association of
   England.
◆ Computer skills: word processing, spreadsheets and
   graphics.
                        References available upon request

Fig. 2.   Sample resumé.

2:4.4 Assessment of education credentials

If you plan to practise in a regulated occupation, check with
the body that regulates that occupation. They may recommend the organisation that you should contact in order to
get your educational credentials assessed (i.e. equivalency

to Canadian Standards, different from licensing issues alone). For more details, see the sections above on **regulated occupations** and **recognition of qualifications in regulated occupations**.

If you intend to work in a non-regulated occupation, there are a number of organisations that can assess your credentials. To find out the relevant contact information, visit the website of the Canadian Information Centre for International Credentials at **www.cicic.ca** and review Factsheet 1.

The purpose of getting your education credentials assessed is to provide a potential employer with a better understanding of your education background. However, you should know that having your credentials assessed does not guarantee that an employer will recognise your credentials. As noted above, in the section on **recognition of qualifications in non-regulated occupations,** an employer has discretion with respect to this aspect.

2:4.5 Retaining the services of an employment agency

There are a number of Canadian employment agencies that can assist you with finding employment in Canada. See Schedule 11 (page 251) for a list of names, addresses and contact information of such agencies.

Whether you are applying for permanent residence under one of the categories available or for a temporary work permit, being familiar with the information contained in this chapter will be of assistance to you. Its overview of the relevant aspects related to working in Canada will help you better understand the chapters to follow.

3

Permanent Residence – Skilled Worker Category

Canadian law defines **skilled workers** as people who may become permanent residents on the basis of their ability to become economically established in Canada.

The skilled worker category is the most important and frequently used method of immigrating to Canada permanently. In order to be admitted under this category, you must first be eligible to apply as a skilled worker. Secondly, in most cases you will be required to show that you have enough funds to move to Canada. Thirdly, you must accumulate enough points (under the system described in section 3:1.3 below), to meet the pass mark; at the time of preparing these materials the pass mark is 67 points.[1]

3:1 REQUIREMENTS FOR QUALIFYING UNDER THIS CATEGORY

3:1.1 Eligibility requirements

In order to have your application assessed by an immigration officer, you must have at least one year of **full-time** (or

---

[1]Please note that the pass mark may fluctuate. Always check the current requirements at **www.cic.gc.ca/skilled**.

full-time equivalent i.e. 37.5 hours/week) **paid work experience**. The work experience must have been acquired in the ten years preceding the making of your application. Also, the work experience must be in Skill Type 0 or Skill Level A or B of the National Occupation Classification (NOC).[2]

In assessing whether or not your work experience falls under Skills Type 0 or Skills Level A or B, ensure that the essential duties of your occupation coincide with the duties listed in the NOC for that occupation (it is substance, not title that counts). Full NOC definitions can be found at **www23.hrdc-drhc.gc.ca**, the web site of Human Resources Development Canada.

Please note that at times certain occupations may be listed as **restricted**. You should also check the list of restricted occupations[3] and see if any of your work experience falls under that list; if you have worked in a restricted occupation, you cannot take into account that work experience for the purposes of your skilled worker application for permanent residence. At this time, there are no restricted occupations.

3:1.2 The funds required

To be accepted as a skilled worker, you must prove that you have the funds required to support yourself and your family, if applicable, after you arrive in Canada.[4] Below is a chart listing the amounts.

---

[2]For more information about the NOC, please see Chapter 2 of this book and Schedule 5 (page 232).
[3]**www.cic.gc.ca**
[4]You do not have to show that you have these funds if you have arranged employment in Canada. See below for more information on arranged employment.

Family members	Funds required (in Canadian dollars)
1	$9,420
2	$11,775
3	$14,645
4	$17,727
5	$19,816
6	$21,905
7 or more	$23,994

3:1.3 Meeting the pass mark

Each skilled worker application is assessed on the basis of **six selection factors** under a **point system**. In order for you to be accepted into Canada as a skilled worker, you must accumulate enough points to meet or exceed the pass mark. As mentioned above, the current pass mark is 67 points.

The six selection factors are: education, language skills, work experience, age, arranged employment and adaptability. The factors are discussed in more detail below. You should note that if you have a spouse or common-law partner, you should calculate his or her points as well. As between you and your spouse/partner, the one who accumulates the most points should be the principal applicant.

Below is a worksheet that can be used to calculate your points.

Factor	Maximum points	Your score
1 Education	25	
2 Language proficiency	24	
3 Work experience	21	
4 Age	10	
5 Arranged employment	10	
6 Adaptability	10	
Total	**100**	

3:1.3.a Factor 1: Education
You can earn a maximum of **25 points** for your education. Two aspects are relevant when it comes to your education: the credentials, i.e. the level of studies you have completed, and the number of years you have spent in school.

Below is a chart with the rules on how points for education are awarded. Before you turn to it, please note the following definitions and comments:

◆ **Full-time studies** means at least 15 hours of instruction per week during the academic year. This includes any period of workplace training that forms part of the course.

◆ **Full-time equivalent studies** means that if you completed a programme of study on a part-time or accelerated basis, in calculating the length of your studies you should count the length of time it would have taken to complete the programme on a full-time basis.

◆ If you have not completed the number of years of study that correspond to your highest educational credential, award yourself points based on the number of years of study. Examples: If you have a Master's degree but have completed only 16 years of full-time study, award yourself 22 points. If you have a four-year Bachelor's degree and have completed 14 or more years of study, award yourself 20 points.

Master's or PhD **and** at least 17 years of full-time or
full-time equivalent study   25

Two or more university degrees at the Bachelor's level
and at least 15 years of full-time or full-time equivalent
study; **or** A three-year diploma, trade certificate or
apprenticeship and at least 15 years of full-time or
full-time equivalent study   22

A university degree of two years or more at the Bachelor's
level, and at least 14 years of full-time or full-time equivalent
study; **or** A two-year diploma, trade certificate or
apprenticeship and at least 14 years of full-time or
full-time equivalent study   20

A one-year university degree at the Bachelor's level
and at least 13 years of full-time or full-time equivalent
study; **or** A one-year diploma, trade certificate or
apprenticeship and at least 13 years of full-time or
full-time equivalent study   15

A one-year diploma, trade certificate or apprenticeship
and at least 12 years of full-time or full-time equivalent
study   12

Secondary school (also called high school)   5

3:1.3.b Factor 2: Language skills

You can earn a maximum of **24 points** for your language
skills. Your skills in reading, writing, listening to and speaking English and/or French are all relevant. If your language
skills extend to both English and French, pick the one
language you are most comfortable with as your first official
language; the other one will be the second official language.

When calculating your language points, remember to add the
points for each relevant aspect: speaking, reading, listening
and writing for both official languages.

There are four proficiency levels that you may have in English or French for the purposes of immigrating to Canada: high, moderate, basic or no proficiency at all. To see the detailed descriptions of each level of proficiency, visit **www.cic.gc.ca** and look for the 'How to assess your language skills' section.

Below is a table that shows you how points are awarded based on your first and second official language proficiency. Please note that if your language skills for two or more of the four aspects are at the basic proficiency level, you cannot accumulate more than two points for those aspects. For example, if your first official language skills in writing, listening and speaking are at the basic level and your reading skills are at the high level, the number of points you would accumulate is 6 (1+1+4).

First official language proficiency	Read	Write	Listen	Speak
High	4	4	4	4
Moderate	2	2	2	2
Basic (maximum of 2 points only)	1	1	1	1
No proficiency	0	0	0	0
Second official language proficiency	**Read**	**Write**	**Listen**	**Speak**
High	2	2	2	2
Moderate	2	2	2	2
Basic (maximum of 2 points only)	1	1	1	1
No proficiency	0	0	0	0

For the purposes of your actual application, you will have to provide conclusive proof of your language abilities.

3:1.3.b(i) Taking a language test

One way of proving your language skills is to take a standardised language test.[5] This is the preferred option. Indeed, most visa posts are insisting on it. Once you receive the results of your test, you can refer to the charts below in order to determine how many points you would receive for your language skills. **Please note that you should go well prepared to the language test; the results will be used as conclusive evidence of your language proficiency.**

International English Language Testing System (IELTS)

| Level | Points (per ability) | Test results for each ability | | | |
		Speaking	Listening	Reading (general training)	Writing (general training)
High	First official language: 4	7.0–9.0	7.0–9.0	7.0–9.0	7.0–9.0
	Second official language: 2	7.0–9.0	7.0–9.0	7.0–9.0	7.0–9.0
Moderate	Either official language: 2	5.0–6.9	5.0–6.9	5.0–6.9	5.0–6.9
Basic	Either official language: 1 (maximum of 2)	4.0–4.9	4.0–4.9	4.0–4.9	4.0–4.9
No	0	Less than 4.0	Less than 4.0	Less than 4.0	Less than 4.0

[5]See Schedule 6 (page 242) for more information about contacting the organisations that administer such tests.

Canadian English Language Proficiency Index Program (CELPIP)

Level	Points (per ability)	Test results for each ability			
		Speaking	Listening	Reading	Writing
High	First official language:				
	4	4H	4H	4H	4H
	5	5	5	5	5
	Second official language:	6	6	6	6
	2	4H	4H	4H	4H
Moderate	Either	5	5	5	5
	official	6	6	6	6
	language:				
	2	3H	3H	3H	3H
Basic	Either official language:	4L	4L	4L	4L
	1	2H	2H	2H	2H
	(maximum of 2)	3L	3L	3L	3L
No	0	0	0	0	0
		1	1	1	1
		2L	2L	2L	2L

Test d'évaluation de français (TEF)

Level	Points (per ability)	Test results for each ability			
		Speaking (expression orale)	Listening (compréhension orale)	Reading (compréhension écrite)	Writing (expression écrite)
High	First official language: 4 Second official language: 2	Level 5 Level 6 (349-450 pts)	Level 5 Level 6 (280-360 pts)	Level 5 Level 6 (233-300 pts)	Level 5 Level 6 (349-450 pts)
Moderate	Either official language: 2	Level 4 (271-348 pts)	Level 4 217-279 pts)	Level 4 (181-232 pts)	Level 4 (271-348 pts)

Basic	Either official language: 1 (maximum of 2)	Level 3 (181-270 pts)	Level 3 (145-216 pts)	Level 3 (121-180 pts)	Level 3 (181-270 pts)
No	0	Level 0 Level 1 Level 2 (0-180 pts)	Level 0 Level 1 Level 2 0-144 pts)	Level 0 Level 1 Level 2 0-120 pts)	Level 0 Level 1 Level 2 (0-180 pts)

3:1.3.b (ii) Providing supporting documentation

The second way of proving your language skills is to provide a written explanation and supporting documentation regarding your language skills. You may use this avenue if you believe that in your case a language test is not necessary. As noted above, however, despite the questionable legal authority, many visa posts are insisting on the IELTS. You should refer to the detailed descriptions of each level of language of ability (visit **www.cic.gc.ca** and look for the 'How to assess your language skills' section). On the basis of that information ensure that you clearly show in your documentation that you meet those criteria. Below is more information about what to do if you wish to pursue this option in relation to your language skills.

◆ Gather material that supports your claim. This should include:

a) a submission written by you that details your training in, and use of, English and/or French, and

b) official documentation of education in English and/or French.

◆ Submit these documents with your immigration application; please note that if any of these particular documents are missing, the visa office will not contact you to request them, it is your responsibility to include them.

◆ The visa office will **not** interview you to assess your proficiency levels.

If the immigration officer assessing your application is not satisfied that you have the proficiency that you claim to have, s/he will make his or her own assessment on the basis of the information submitted. Your application may be refused if this results in a shortage of points.

The disadvantage with this option is that you will **not** know exactly how many points you will receive for the language factor until after your application is assessed.

3:1.3.c Factor 3: Work experience
You can obtain a maximum of **21 points** for your work experience. However, for work experience to be taken into account, it must meet **all** of the following conditions:

◆ be full-time or full-time equivalent paid work experience (though not necessarily contiguous);

◆ must have been obtained within the ten years preceding the making of your application;

◆ must not have been obtained in a restricted occupation (though no occupation is currently listed as restricted);

◆ have been obtained in occupations listed in Skill Type 0 or Skill Level A or B of the NOC.

For more information about the last two requirements, see section 3:1.1 above. If your experience meets these tests, points will be awarded as follows:

Years of experience	Points
1	15
2	17
3	19
4+	21

3:1.3.d Factor 4: Age

You can obtain a maximum of **10 points** under this category. The points are given for your age at the time the application is received by the visa office.

Age	Total points
16 or under	0
17	2
18	4
19	6
20	8
21–49	10
50	8
51	6
52	4
53	2
54 and over	0

3:1.3.e Factor 5: Arranged employment

You can obtain a maximum of **10 points** under this selection factor. **Arranged employment** means employment you know at the time of making your permanent residence application that you would have if your application were accepted and you came to Canada. Below is a chart showing how points are awarded under this selection factor.

If:	And:	Points
You are currently working in Canada on a temporary work permit[6] (including sectoral confirmations)	• Your work permit is valid for 12 or more months **after** the date you apply for a permanent resident visa, and • Your employer offered to give you a permanent job if your application is successful.	10
You are currently working in Canada in a job that is HRSDC[7] confirmation-exempt under an international agreement or a significant benefit category (e.g. intra-company transferee)[8]	• Your work permit is valid for 12 or more months **after** the date you apply for a permanent resident visa, and • Your employer offered to give you a permanent job if your application is successful.	10
You do not currently have a work permit and you do not intend to work in Canada before you have been issued a permanent resident visa.	• You have a full-time job offer that has been approved for arranged employment by HRSDC;[9] please note that the approval is based on the assessment of the following factors: the genuineness of the offer of employment, whether the wages and working conditions of the employment would be sufficient to attract and retain Canadians, and whether the employment is full-time and not seasonal. • Your employer has made an offer to give you a permanent job if your application is successful. • You meet all required Canadian licensing or regulatory standards associated with the job.	10

[6]For more information about work permits, including sectoral confirmations, see Chapter 7.
[7]HRSDC stands for Human Resource and Skills Development Canada.
[8]See Chapter 7.
[9]You cannot arrange for an HRSDC confirmation, your employer must do this. For additional information and sample form to be used by employers, see Figure 3, pages 37–40. Also, please note that HRSDC will confirm job offers for occupations listed in Skill Type 0 or Skill Level A or B of the NOC.

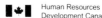 Human Resources   Développement des
Development Canada   ressources humaines Canada

Arranged Employment Application for Skilled Workers
Information Sheet

These procedures do not apply to offers of employment for positions in the Province of Québec

ARRANGED EMPLOYMENT OPINION

As part of the permanent resident application process, HRDC provides an opinion on the genuineness of an offer of permanent employment made by an employer to a foreign national, when the foreign national will not be working in Canada before receiving a permanent resident visa. The opinion is based on whether:

1. the offer of employment is genuine;
2. the wages and working conditions of the employment would be sufficient to attract and retain Canadians; and
3. the employment is full-time and not seasonal.

FILL OUT THIS APPLICATION ONLY IF:

You are an employer (or an authorized third party) who has made an offer of permanent employment to a foreign national who is a skilled worker and

1. the position is not located in the Province of Québec;
2. the position offered is full-time;
3. the foreign national does not intend to work in Canada until his/her application for permanent residence is approved and he/she is issued a permanent resident visa; and
4. the position offered falls within the National Occupation Classification (NOC) skill levels 0, A or B. As a general rule, these positions require two years or more of post secondary education or on the job training in order to qualify. More detailed information on job classifications can be found at http://www23.hrdc-drhc.gc.ca/2001/e/generic/welcome.shtml

Please ensure the following documents are attached to the application:

1. The offer of permanent employment to the foreign national, on company letterhead, signed by the person responsible for hiring employees. The letter must state the length of time the offer of employment is open, the title of the position that is offered and the salary to be paid to the prospective employee.
2. Copies of remittance forms issued by CCRA itemizing source deductions for the previous 12 months (form number PD7A).
3. Evidence that the business has been in operation for more than one year. This can be shown by submitting any one of the following documents: business licenses spanning more than 12 months; CCRA T4 Summary of Deductions for the previous year; commercial lease agreement for the business location.

Employers will be advised in writing of HRDC's opinion.

EMP5275 (10-02)E   Aussi disponible en français EMP 5275F

Fig. 3.   Arranged employment application.

Please Print

PROTECTED WHEN COMPLETED - B

ARRANGED EMPLOYMENT APPLICATION FOR SKILLED WORKERS

EMPLOYER INFORMATION

Business name		Name of Business Owner		

Business Address:

Number, Street and Post Office Box Number	City	Province	Postal Code

Is this a head office? ☐ Yes ☐ No	Canada Customs and Revenue Agency (CCRA) business number	Please provide copies of CCRA Remittance Forms (PD7A) showing that the business has paid source deductions for employees over the past 12 months.

Date business started: yyyy / mm / dd	Website	Number of employees in Canada	Telephone Number ( ) –

Describe the principal business activity:

Location of employment of prospective employee if different from employer's address:

Number, Street and Post Office Box Number	City	Province	Postal Code

Please provide evidence that the business has been in operation for over one year. Documents may include: Business licenses, CCRA T4 Summary of Deductions for the previous tax year, and Commercial lease agreement.

CONTACT INFORMATION

Name of Business Contact	Address if different from above:			
	Number, Street and Post Office Box Number	City	Province	Postal Code

Job Title	Telephone Number ( ) –	Fax Number ( ) –	E-mail

THIRD PARTY INFORMATION *(if applicable)

Third Party Agent authorized to act for employer	Company name of Agent

Address:

Number, Street and Post Office Box Number	City	Province	Postal Code

Telephone Number ( ) –	Fax Number ( ) –	E-mail	Website

* If you are a third party agent acting on behalf of an employer, written authorization from the employer to act on his/her behalf is required and should
• normally be presented on the employer's original company letterhead;
• be signed by an official with signing authority for the employer;
• specifically authorize the agent to act on the employer's behalf; and
• state any limitations of authority to act on the employer's behalf (duration, specific situations etc.)

HRDC reserves the right to contact the employer directly if necessary.

Fig. 3. continued.

INFORMATION ON JOB OFFER

Occupation

Job title within your organization

Requirements of the job. Provide details:

a) provincial / territorial accreditation, certification, licensing, or registration requirements:

b) educational / knowledge requirements:

c) experience:

d) skills:

e) language requirements:

☐ English ☐ French ☐ Other If "Other", please explain:

Duties the employee will perform and any working conditions specific to the job:

Is this work seasonal in nature? ☐ No ☐ Yes If yes, please explain:

What is the expiry date (if any) of this offer of indeterminate employment?
yyyy / mm / dd

This application must be accompanied by a copy of the original indeterminate offer of employment to the foreign national, on company letterhead signed by an authorized Official.

Salary (not including gratuities, commission, room and board):

$ _____ per hour $ _____ per day $ _____ per month $ _____ per year

Number of hours of work per day

Number of days of work per week

Other benefits:

gratuities $ _____ bonuses $ _____ commissions $ _____ room & board $ _____ paid holidays _____

☐ disability insurance ☐ medical insurance ☐ dental insurance ☐ pension Other: _____

FOREIGN WORKER INFORMATION

Family name

Given Name(s)

☐ Male ☐ Female

Date of birth
yyyy / mm / dd

Country of birth

Citizenship

Current address of prospective employee:

Number, Street and Post Office Box Number	City	Province	Country	Postal Code

Fig. 3. continued.

FOREIGN WORKER INFORMATION (Continued)

At which immigration post will the prospective employee likely be processed?

Is the prospective employee related to anyone in the organization? ☐ No ☐ Yes

DECLARATION OF EMPLOYER

I intend to offer _____

(name of prospective employee)

indeterminate employment in the position described above upon approval of his/her application for permanent resident status.

I understand that personal information about the prospective employee will be shared by Human Resources Development Canada(HRDC) with Citizenship and Immigration Canada(CIC) and may be shared with other federal/provincial/territorial departments and their agencies to support the application of the prospective employee for permanent residency (landed immigrant status).

I also understand that all other information found in the application (except personal information about the prospective employee) will be shared by HRDC with CIC and may be shared with federal/provincial/territorial departments and their agencies as well as municipal governments, unions and associations and other appropriate organizations to ensure employers are meeting the requirements to hire skilled workers under immigration legislation.

This information may be used for research, evaluation and/or policy analysis.

I/We certify that the information contained in this application is true and accurate.

_____   _____

Signature of Authorized Official or Third Party Representative   Title of Authorized Official

_____   _____

Name of Employer   Date

INFORMATION FOR EMPLOYERS

Completion of this form is voluntary; however failure to provide any of the requested information may mean points for arranged employment, as outlined in the Immigration and Refugee Protection Regulations, will not be awarded to the prospective employee. You may submit a request to HRDC to view the information provided on the form pursuant to the Privacy Act. Instructions for making formal requests are provided in the publication, Info Source, copies of which are available at Human Resource Centres of Canada or on the web at: http://infosource.gc.ca/
When requesting information, refer to Personal Information Bank number HRDC PPU 440.

**Please forward this application to the nearest
Human Resources Centre of Canada (HRCC) responsible for processing skilled worker applications.
For the list of HRCCs consult the National Foreign Worker website at:**

**http:www.hrdc-drhc.gc.ca/hrib/lmd-dmt/fw-te/
or
consult the blue pages of your telephone directory under Government of Canada. Once an Officer approves this
application, the employer will be notified. The prospective employee must then apply to
Citizenship and Immigration Canada.**

Fig. 3. continued.

3:1.3.f Factor 6: Adaptability

You can obtain a maximum of **10 points** under this selection factor even if you appear to achieve more. The points are awarded on the basis of your experience and/or that of your spouse or common-law partner. Please note that points for each element can be awarded only once, either for you or your spouse or common-law partner.

Adaptability criteria

1. Spouse or common-law partner's level of education:
- Secondary school (high school) diploma or less: **0 points**
- A one-year diploma, trade certificate, apprenticeship, or university degree and at least 12 years of full-time or full-time equivalent studies: **3 points**
- A diploma, trade certificate, apprenticeship, or university degree of two years or more and at least 14 years of full-time or full-time equivalent studies: **4 points**
- A Master's or PhD and at least 17 years of full-time or full-time equivalent studies: **5 points**

2. Previous study in Canada:
- You or your accompanying spouse or common-law partner studied at a post-secondary institution in Canada for at least two years on a full-time basis. This must have been done after the age of 17 and with a valid study permit. **5 points**

3. Previous work in Canada:
- You or your accompanying spouse or common-law partner completed a minimum of one year of full-time work in Canada on a valid work permit. **5 points**

4. Arranged employment:

◆ You earned points under Factor 5: Arranged Employment. **5 points**

5. Relatives in Canada:

◆ You or your accompanying spouse or common-law partner has a relative (parent, grandparent, child, grandchild, child of a parent, sibling, child of a grandparent, aunt/uncle, or grandchild of a parent, niece or nephew) who lives in Canada and is a Canadian citizen or permanent resident. **5 points**

3:1.4 Summary of factors and general considerations

If after counting your points you have met or exceeded the pass mark, then you may qualify for immigration to Canada as a skilled worker. Please note that it is always the immigration official's assessment of the points you are entitled to that prevails if there is a difference between the points as assessed by you and as assessed by the official.

If, on the other hand, after counting your points your total score is less than the pass mark, it means that you are not likely to qualify for immigration to Canada as a skilled worker.

However, you should know that even if you do not appear to achieve 67 points or more, you may nevertheless apply if you believe that there are other factors that would help you to become economically established in Canada. You should include a detailed letter with your application explaining these factors. Include any documents that support your claim.

In terms of the options you have if you do not meet the pass mark, they include working towards improving your language skills or education, seeking to obtain arranged employment and checking to see if you might qualify for the other categories of permanent residence applications, discussed in more detail in Chapters 5 and 6.

3:2 THE APPLICATION FOR PERMANENT RESIDENCE

As mentioned in Chapter 1, the forms to be included in an application for permanent residence can be downloaded, together with the instructions accompanying them, from the site of CIC at **www.cic.gc.ca**. In the case of skilled worker permanent residence applications, there are also visa office specific instructions which you must ensure you obtain from the relevant visa office, as highlighted in Chapter 1. The Appendix at the end of the book provides you with a sample of such visa office specific instructions (the London office).

3:2.1 Inclusion of a resumé

In addition to the basic documents as noted in the relevant checklist (contained in the visa office Specific Instructions booklet), one useful, often pivotal document is a resumé, which puts it all into perspective. In Chapter 2 we briefly discussed the issue of the resumé to be used for job searching purposes. Though the information may be generally the same, a resumé to be included in an application for permanent residence may be slightly different from a resumé you submit to an employer, there may be different points to stress.

The resumé for immigration authorities should be longer than two pages. Your focus in drafting should be on providing good descriptions of the duties you have had in the past. It is important to remember the following:

◆ organise the duties in a logical way;

◆ use clear language and keep the use of technical terms to a minimum;

◆ do not present the same duty in different ways; decide what the substance of the duty was and use the simplest description of it;

◆ do not list everything that you did at a particular job; include mostly the tasks that were specific and central to your position.

You can use as a reference the NOC job titles and descriptions. However, you should ensure that your resumé does not just reproduce the NOC descriptions. If it does, you will lose credibility with the immigration officer assessing your application and you may receive fewer points for your work experience than you may be entitled to. For a sample resumé to be included in your application, see Figure 4.

3:3 CONCLUSION

An application for permanent residence may be the pivotal part in your life; it is about more than just filling in forms. Make sure you understand what CIC is looking for and give it to them through the application proccess. Knowledge is power and the power to know what a visa office must/cannot/might consider should be behind your application. Don't leave anything to chance.

JILL DOE
14 Blackburn Road
Suffolk JW2 46X
England
jdoe@e-mail.com
Tel.: 44-1473-290-821/ Mob.: 44-1473-290-821

NURSE

OBJECTIVE
Seeking a full-time permanent or contract position with a
well-established health care organisation in the Toronto area.

KEY SKILLS
- Providing qualitative patient care addressing physical,
  emotional, psycho-social and spiritual needs
- Providing nursing care in hospitals, clinics, long term care
  facilities and through home visits
- Providing community health services or referring patients
  to community health organisations
- Maintaining a safe, neat and clean environment for
  patients and personnel
- Assessing a patient's condition by evaluating signs and
  symptoms and monitoring patient status
- Administering medication and delivering medical
  treatment as prescribed by hospital staff or physicians
- Compiling data and preparing case records, incident
  reports, progress reports and other paperwork
- Assisting with surgery and other medical procedures and
  providing post-operative care

EXPERIENCE
02/00 – Present: Nurse, Toronto General Hospital
Admit patients, including patients in labour and patients
transferred from the emergency room or post-operative
wards. Compile data to be included in patient medical
records. Provide qualitative care to ante-natal and post-natal
patients. Assess newborns and their mothers upon admission
and during their stay. Design, implement and evaluate
programs of care for newborns and mothers. Provide
post-operative care. Refer patients to be discharged to health
centres in their communities.

Fig. 4.   Sample resumé.

12/90 – 02/00: Nurse, Chicago General Hospital
Monitored the status of patients. Provided qualitative patient care by administering the prescribed medical treatment in a safe, timely and effective manner. Maintained a therapeutic environment. Adopted and implemented safety precautions such as infection control measures. Provided community health services. Assisted with surgery and other medical procedures.

EDUCATION
1990: Bachelor of Science in Nursing
University of Toronto, Toronto

PROFESSIONAL QUALIFICATIONS
1990: Registered Nurse

PROFESSIONAL TRAINING
2000: General Nursing Orientation
1998: Charting and Clinical Documentation
1996: Basic Life Support
1990: Nursing Process

INTERESTS
Reading and golfing.

REFERENCES
Available upon request.

Fig. 4.   continued.

4

Permanent Residence – Family Category

Canadian permanent residents and citizens can sponsor close relatives or family members from abroad[1] who want to become Canadian permanent residents.

4:1 WHO CAN BE SPONSORED

The following categories of people can be sponsored:

♦ spouses, common-law or conjugal partners 16 years of age or older;

♦ parents and grandparents;

♦ dependent children, including adopted children;

♦ children under 18 years of age whom you intend to adopt;

♦ children under guardianship;

---

[1]In some cases, notably spouses/common-law partners, sponsorship can be made inland for sponsorees physically present in Canada. This is a separate topic, not covered in this book.

◆ brothers, sisters, nephews, nieces or grandchildren who are orphans, under the age of 18 and not married or in a common-law relationship; or

◆ you may also sponsor one relative of any age if you do not have an aunt, uncle or a family member from the list above who you could sponsor or who is already a Canadian citizen or permanent resident.

4:2 WHAT DOES IT MEAN TO SPONSOR?

When someone in Canada sponsors one or more of the above persons they take it upon themselves (by signing an undertaking with the Minister of Citizenship and Immigration) to be financially responsible for the person(s) sponsored (the sponsoree(s)).

The undertaking to sponsor is an unconditional promise of support. Changes in the life of the sponsoree, such as the granting of Canadian citizenship, divorce, separation, relationship breakdown or moving to another province do not cancel the undertaking, which will remain in force even if the sponsor's financial situation deteriorates.

The **sponsorship period** varies in duration from three to ten years, depending on the age and/or the relationship between the sponsor and the sponsored person(s). During the sponsorship period, it is expected that the persons sponsored will not seek social assistance, in view of the responsibility the sponsor has taken.

If a sponsored person does apply for federal, provincial

or municipal assistance during the sponsorship period, the sponsor:

◆ will be considered to be in default of their obligations;

◆ may have to repay the financial aid received by the sponsored person(s);

◆ will not be allowed to sponsor other members of the family class until the amounts outstanding are paid back to the authorities who provided the sponsored persons with assistance.

4:3 REQUIREMENTS THAT THE SPONSOR MUST MEET

If a Canadian citizen/resident wishes to sponsor any of the above-listed relatives or family members, they may be eligible to do so if they meet the following requirements:

◆ they are 18 years of age or older;

◆ they are a Canadian citizen or permanent resident;

◆ they reside in Canada (except in the case of Canadian citizens sponsoring spouses and common law spouses);

◆ they sign an undertaking, promising to provide for the basic requirements of the person(s) being sponsored;

◆ they and the sponsored person(s) sign an agreement that confirms that each party understands his or her mutual obligations and responsibilities;

◆ they, the sponsor, have an income that is at least equal to the minimum necessary income (they must, in this regard, provide proof of their financial situation for the past 12 months).

The **minimum necessary income** (see below for the amounts at the time of the preparation of these materials) is the income necessary to support the group of persons consisting of:

◆ the sponsor and their family members, whether living with you or not;

◆ the person(s) to be sponsored;

◆ every other person that the sponsor may have sponsored in the past where an undertaking is still in effect or not yet in effect;

◆ every other person for whom the sponsor, has co-signed an undertaking that is still in effect (see below for more information on co-signers);

◆ every person not mentioned above for whom the sponsor's spouse or common-law partner has given or co-signed an undertaking that is still in effect or not yet in effect, if their spouse or common-law partner is co-signing the current sponsorship undertaking.

Please note that if the sponsor's income is too low, it is possible to have a spouse or common-law partner as **co-signer** in the sponsorship. The co-signer must:

◆ meet the same eligibility requirements as the sponsor;

◆ agree to co-sign your undertaking; and

◆ agree to be responsible for the basic requirements of the person(s) to be sponsored for the validity period of the undertaking. The co-signer will be equally liable if the obligations undertaken by the sponsor are not performed.

Minimum income requirements

Size of family unit	Minimum necessary income
1 person (the sponsor)	$18,841
2 persons	$23,551
3 persons	$29,290
4 persons	$35,455
5 persons	$39,633
6 persons	$43,811
7 persons	$47,988
For each additional person	$4,178

4:3.1 Who cannot sponsor

A person will not be eligible to sponsor in a number of circumstances, including the following:

◆ if they are in default of a previous sponsorship undertaking (i.e. person(s) who have been sponsored in the past have received social assistance during the validity period of the undertaking and the sponsor, not repaid the full amount of the social assistance received by the sponsor(s));

◆ if they are in default of an immigration loan (they have received an immigration loan and have unpaid arrears on it);

◆ if they are in default of court ordered support payment obligations;

◆ if they are in prison;

◆ if they are in receipt of social assistance for a reason other than disability.

In the first three situations mentioned above, to regain the right to sponsor, the sponsor will have to make the payments they are under an obligation to make.

4:4 THE STAGES OF THE PROCESS

The application process varies depending on who is being sponsored.

4:4.1 Sponsoring a spouse, common-law or conjugal partner, or a dependent child

If the Canadian citizen/resident is applying to sponsor a spouse, common-law or conjugal partner, or a dependent child, the process will be faster than in the case of other family members or close relatives. The sponsor will send[2] the sponsorship application, together with the application for immigration of the person(s) they wish to sponsor. Please note that the sponsor will pay all the fees.[3] Portions of the fees are refundable in certain circumstances.[4]

If all the sponsorship requirements are met, the application for immigration to Canada of the person(s) being sponsored will be sent to the appropriate visa office abroad for processing. That office may accept or refuse the application.

[2]The application must be sent to the Case Processing Centre (CPC) – Mississauga, P.O. Box 6100, Station A, Mississauga ON L5A 4H4.
[3]See Schedule 4 (page 228) for the applicable fees.
[4]For example, if a sponsorship application is not approved. For more information on this topic, see the Guide accompanying the forms.

4:4.2 Sponsoring other family members or close relatives

In the first stage, the Canadian citizen or permanent resident will submit a sponsorship application.[5] The sponsor will have to pay the fees associated with this part of the process.[6] If the application to sponsor is approved, the CPC will inform the sponsor of that, and provide them with an application package for the use of the person(s) to be sponsored, who will apply for permanent residence at the relevant visa office.

4:5 WHAT HAPPENS IF THE SPONSORSHIP APPLICATION IS REFUSED

It is important to notify the CPC (by ticking a box on the Application to Sponsor and Undertaking form) of the sponsor's intent to withdraw the sponsorship application in the event that they are found ineligible to sponsor.

They must do so before the immigration authorities begin processing the application for permanent residence of the sponsoree(s). There are two main reasons for that. First, if you do not do so, you will lose the right to be refunded some of the fees. Secondly, if you do not qualify as a sponsor and you have not notified the CPC of your intent to withdraw, the application of the person you are sponsoring will be processed. The likely outcome is that the application for permanent residence will be rejected.

If the sponsor does not qualify and has chosen to withdraw their sponsorship application in such circumstances, the

---

[5]The application must again be sent to the CPC – Mississauga, P.O. Box 6100, Station A, Mississauga ON L5A 4H4.
[6]See Schedule 4 (page 228) for the applicable fees.

fees will be refunded. There will be no decision on the application for permanent residence of the person(s) to be sponsored. If the sponsor resolves the situation leading to their ineligibility, they can reapply as a sponsor at a later date.

4:6 WHAT HAPPENS IF THE APPLICATION OF THE PERSON TO BE SPONSORED IS REFUSED

There are a number of reasons why the application for permanent residence of the person(s) to be sponsored might be refused. They include cases where the immigration authorities conclude that the relationship between the sponsor and the sponsoree is for immigration purposes only, or where the sponsoree(s) is inadmissible due to a criminal record or a serious illness.

Both the sponsor and the sponsoree(s) will be informed in writing of the reasons for refusal. The sponsoree(s) will be notified of the rights to appeal and be provided with the instructions of how to commence an appeal.

4:7 CANCELLING THE UNDERTAKING

If the sponsor decides that they no longer wish to be a sponsor, they must write to CPC before the sponsoree(s) are issued permanent resident visas. If the visas have already been issued, the promise undertaken by the sponsor and the co-signer, if applicable, will be valid for the term of the undertaking.

4:8 OTHER RELEVANT CHANGES

If a co-signer withdraws their support for the sponsorship application, either or both the sponsor and co-signer must write a letter to the CPC and the relevant visa office before the permanent residence visas are issued to the sponsoree(s). As well, they will have to send amended copies of the sponsorship application and agreement, initialled by both signer and co-signer, removing the co-signer's support.

The sponsor's financial situation will be reassessed, and if they do not meet the financial requirements on their own, the application for permanent residence will be refused.

Please also note that the sponsor, must inform CPC without delay if, following the making of an application, their family status changes (i.e. if there is a marriage, a divorce, a birth or death) or if their contact information changes. In their correspondence with CPC, the file number should be included; it can be found at the top of the correspondence CPC will send to acknowledge the receipt of the application.

4:9 A COMMENT ON THE SPONSOREE'S DEPENDANTS

Please note that if you have a child, even if the child is in the sole custody of your former spouse, you will have to include the child on your application for permanent residence. However, the child does not need to be examined if you do not have custody or responsibility for the child because of a written agreement or a court order.

It is important to note that if a child is not examined, regardless of the changes to custody or living circumstances, you will not be able to sponsor him or her as a family member in the future.

5

Permanent Residence – Provincial Nominee Programs

5:1 INTRODUCTION

In Chapters 3 and 4 we discussed the process of immigrating to Canada by applying directly to the federal immigration authorities. Obtaining permanent residence under a Provincial Nominee Program (PNP) is a two-step process. Initially, an application has to be made to the provincial/ territorial immigration authorities. If your skill is needed in that province/territory, and the other requirements specific to their PNP are met, you will be nominated and issued a Nomination Certificate (NC). With such a certificate you can then move to the second stage of the process, which is applying for permanent residence to the federal immigration authorities. **It is important to note that being nominated under a PNP is not a guarantee that you will receive a permanent resident visa** (though certainly it virtually always will lead to such a visa). Citizenship and Immigration Canada (CIC) may still assess the matter based on the relevant provincial–federal agreement[1]. Before you are

[1] The PNPs are established under agreements between the Federal Government of Canada and the individual provinces.

57

issued an immigration visa you will have to meet all federal statutory requirements, including but not limited to health, criminal and security checks.

It is important to note that each PNP has a particular set of eligibility criteria. The programs are also structured differently, some having more than one category of admission. For example, the province of Alberta accepts candidates only under the Skilled Worker category; on the other hand, Prince Edward Island has a Skilled Worker category, as well as an Immigrant Entrepreneurs one.

There are, however, a number of elements that all PNPs have in common.

5:1.1 PNP common elements

The first and most important common element of all PNPs is that if you obtain permanent residence through one province's program, upon coming to Canada you are expected to establish yourself in that province. In some cases you will actually be required to sign an undertaking that you will reside in that province.

Second, each province can only accept a limited number of people each year under its individual PNP. Therefore, even if you meet the requirements, you may not be nominated if the province has reached the maximum number of candidates for that year.

5:1.1.a Common elements relating to the skilled worker category

If you apply under the Skilled Worker category of a PNP, the application process will involve a specific employer making you an offer of employment. The provincial authorities will assess the employer and the position the employer wishes to make available to foreign workers by looking at whether:

◆ the offer is for permanent full-time employment;

◆ the position meets provincial employment and wage standards;

◆ the position is in conflict with existing collective bargaining agreements.

If the employer is approved under the PNP, the employer can then recruit a foreign worker. An applicant to whom an offer of employment has been made can apply to the province for nomination. Their application will be assessed on the basis of:

◆ related work experience;

◆ whether the individual meets the qualifications as required by the employer and recognised by industry standards/associations;

◆ the applicant's ability to settle in the province.

Due to the scope of this book, this chapter will not cover all the existing PNPs, but rather highlight some of the more active ones, specifically the Alberta, British Columbia and Manitoba PNPs. A list of all PNP contact information is provided at the end of this chapter. The basic requirements for PNPs are shown in Figure 5.

	AB	BC	MN	NFLD	PEI	SK	NB	YK
Employer Driven (i.e. application submitted by Employer)	Y	Y	N	N	N	N	N	N/A
Recruitment Effort	Y	Y	N	N	N	Y	N Critical Impact and work permit	N/A
Shortage List	N	N but Industry specific	Y	Y	Y	Y	Y	N/A
Job Offer	Y	Y	Y But only semi-skilled workers & international students	Y	Y	Y Critical Impact only	Y	N/A
International Students	N	Y	Y	N	N	N	N	N/A
Adult Dependants	N	N	Y	N	N	N	N	N/A
Provincial Application Fee	N	Y Bus. Skills: $3000. Project: $1000 per Key staff	N	Y $1000	Y $1500	N	N	N
PNP Business Program	N	Y	Y	Y	Y	Y	Y	Y
Business Case or Plan Required?	Y	Y Bus. Skills Category only	N	N	N	Y Farmers & Business	Y	Y
Investment (CAD)	N/A	$1M	$150,000	Not Fixed	$15K or $250K	Not Fixed	Not Fixed	$150,000
Net Worth	N/A	$2M	$250,000	Not Fixed	Not Fixed	Not Fixed except $500K for Farmers	Not Fixed	$250,000
Exploratory Visit	N	Strongly Recommended	Y	N	Y	Y	Y	Y
Prior Ownership, Business and/or Management Expertise	N	Y Business	Y Business		Y	Y Farmers & Business	Y	Y

Fig. 5. Provincial Nominee Programs – Basic Requirements.

5:2 THE ALBERTA PNP

The Alberta PNP has only one category, that of Skilled Worker. The programme is 'employer-driven', meaning that it is the employer who has to apply and seek approval to recruit foreign candidates. The employer will have to submit a 'business case' that will demonstrate the company's need for the position, and its inability to fill the position with a qualified Canadian resident. More precisely, the employer will have to prove that there is a shortage of qualified workers for the position in Alberta.

See Figure 6 for a sample Employer Application, and for a list of the supporting documents that the employer has to submit.

Once the employer has been approved and has found a candidate for the position, the employer must make an offer of employment to the candidate and enter into a contract with the latter. The employer must then submit the contract and the completed Guaranteed Job Offer Form (Figure 7) to the provincial immigration authorities. The potential nominee will submit the completed Skilled Worker/Professional form, a sample of which can be found in Figure 8.

For more information about the Alberta PNP, please visit **www.alberta-canada.com**, and contact:

Provincial Nominee Program
Economic Immigration
Alberta Economic Development
4th Floor, Commerce Place, 10155-102 St.,
Edmonton, Alberta, Canada T5J 4L6

**ALBERTA PROVINCIAL
NOMINEE PROGRAM**

Employer Application

Employer Application: ABPNP 001

An employer's application to have a skilled worker nominated for immigration under the Alberta Provincial Nominee Program will be considered if the employment offer:

- Is for permanent, full-time position(s) in Alberta;
- Meets provincial employment and wage standards;
- Is made to an individual who meets the required qualifications for the position; and
- Does not conflict with existing collective bargaining agreements

Please note:
This application must be completed in full with accompanying attachments, failure to comply will result in a delay in processing.

Please indicate the Ministry and individual contacted that assisted you with the PNP application process:

☐ Alberta Economic Development   Ministry Specialist: _____

☐ Alberta Agriculture, Food and Rural Development   Ministry Specialist: _____

☐ Alberta Innovation and Science   Ministry Specialist: _____

☐ Alberta Health and Wellness   Ministry Specialist: _____

☐ Other: _____

A. Employer Information

1. Employer Name: Name of Employer Contact:

Telephone: Facsimile: E-mail: Website:

Mailing Address: City/Town: Postal Code:

2. Head office (if applicable):
Mailing Address: Head office (if applicable):
City/Town: Head office (if applicable):
Postal Code:

Head office (if applicable):
Telephone: Head office (if applicable):
Facsimile: Head office (if applicable):
E-mail: Head office (if applicable):
Website:

3. Corporate registry number: 4. WCB account number (if not applicable, please clarify):

GOVERNMENT OF ALBERTA
CANADA

Fig. 6. Sample employer application.

**ALBERTA PROVINCIAL
NOMINEE PROGRAM**

5. Type of Company: (provide a concise description of the firm's type of industry, goods manufactured or services provided and **attach** information on the business

FOR OFFICE USE ONLY   NAICS:

6. Year business established: _____

7. Number of employees: in Alberta _____   Other: _____

8. Markets:
☐ Canada: Specify Province: _____
☐ United States: Specify State: _____
☐ International: Specify Country: _____

9. Have you previously applied to any other Provincial Nominee Programs? If so, please indicate when, Province and number of nominee(s):
_____
_____
_____

B. Occupation Information:
Is this an occupation that is:
☐ a ministry supported critical skill occupation

☐ filled by a Temporary Foreign Worker

How many Provincial Nominee Program (PNP) certificates are you seeking: _____

1. Occupation: FOR OFFICE USE ONLY
   (use separate applications for each occupation)   NOC:

2. Position Description: (attach detailed position description and required qualifications)

3. Is this a permanent and full-time position: ☐ YES   ☐ NO

4. Salary Range:

5. Education requirements:
   ☐ University   ☐ Trade School/College   ☐ Other: (please specify)_____

6. Canadian/Alberta industry/association standards required:
   ☐ Association standards   ☐ Industry standards
   ☐ Journeyman standards   ☐ Other: _____

7. Methodology for assessment and recognition of foreign credentials: (provide as a separate attachment)

8. Union: ☐ No   ☐ Yes If yes, please specify:_____

9. Language fluency required for position:

English:	Read	Speak	Write	French:	Read	Speak	Write
Fluent:	☐	☐	☐	Fluent:	☐	☐	☐
Well:	☐	☐	☐	Well:	☐	☐	☐
Functional:	☐	☐	☐	Functional:	☐	☐	☐

Fig. 6. continued.

**ALBERTA PROVINCIAL
NOMINEE PROGRAM**

10. Rationale for need of this occupation: (use separate sheet if required)

_____
_____
_____
_____

11. Benefits accruing to Albertans and Alberta labour market: (use separate sheet if required)

_____
_____
_____
_____

12. Recruitment Activity:

(a) Is this a new position:　☐ Yes　　☐ No
If YES, please indicate reason for new position: (use separate sheet if required)

_____
_____
_____

(b) How long has this position been vacant? How long have you advertised? (specify months)

vacant: _____　　advertised: _____

(c) Where and for how long have you tried to recruit for this position in Alberta/Canada? (Please attach supporting documents)

(d) If you have not recruited for this position, please explain

_____
_____
_____
_____

(e) Have you contacted any of Alberta Economic Development 's international offices? If so, please note which one(s):

_____

(f) Recruitment Plan: **Please attach a recruitment plan which details who, where and how this recruitment process will be undertaken**

13. Employer's employee benefit plan and retention program: (provide as a separate attachment)

C. Alberta Provincial Nominee Program:

How did you learn about the Alberta Provincial Nominee Program? (Please check all boxes that apply)

☐ AB Promotional Material　　☐ PNP Website　　　　☐ Industry Association
☐ Government Department (please specify)_____
　　Other (please specify) _____

Fig. 6. continued.

**ALBERTA PROVINCIAL
NOMINEE PROGRAM**

D. Authorization:

I certify that the information provided for this application is true and correct. I certify that to my knowledge, the employment of the position does not conflict with any existing bargaining agreements, the settlement of any labour dispute or the employment of a person involved in such a dispute. I understand that the information in this form may be used for purposes of evaluating the Alberta Provincial Nominee Program, and I affirm that the employer named above agrees to be contacted in the future for purposes of evaluating the Alberta Provincial Nominee Program.

If this application form and material has been completed by my Agent, on my behalf, I authorize my Agent to provide the completed form and material to the Alberta Government. I further authorize my Agent and the Alberta Government to discuss the contents of my application, or additional information of this type, for the purposes described in this form.

Name of Authorized Signing Officer: (please print)   Title of Authorized Signing Officer:

Signature of Authorized Signing Officer: Date Signed: (dd/mm/yyyy)

The personal information that you provide on this form is collected under the authority of Section 8 of the *Government Organization Act* (RSA 2000) and Section 33 (a) and (c) of the *Freedom of Information and Protection of Privacy Act* (RSA 2000). The information will be used to contact you regarding your companys application under the Alberta Provincial Nominee Program. If you have any questions about the collection of this information you can contact the Provincial Nominee Program (PNP), Alberta Economic Development, 4th Floor, Commerce Place, 10155—102 Street, Edmonton, Alberta, Canada T5J 4L6. Telephone: (780) 427-6764; Facsimile: (780) 427-6560.

If a person other than the applicant has prepared this form, please complete the following:
This form has been prepared by:

☐ lawyer   Name: _____
                  Address: _____
☐ immigration consultant   _____
                  Telephone: _____
☐ other:_____   E-mail: _____

CHECKLIST:

The following **documentation is required** by the Alberta **Provincial Nominee** Program in order to process your application **(for further information about required documents please see instructions included in the Employer Application Kit, Procedure -- Step 2):**

☐ Completed application form. Employer Application (ABPNP 001)
☐ Information on the employer's operations including most recent financial statements
☐ Supporting documents on skill shortage including Recruitment Activity for in-Alberta labour requirements
☐ Copy of company training human resource plan
☐ Copy of detailed position description including qualifications required
☐ Methodology for credential recognition or assessment (how will an applicants credentials be assessed and how will applicant obtain credentials for employment in Alberta)
☐ Copy of HRDC application, validation letter, and employment authorization, if occupation filled by a Temporary Foreign Worker

Send **completed application form** and accompanying attachments to:

Alberta Provincial **Nominee** Program
Alberta Economic **Development**
4th Floor, 10155 — 102 Street
Edmonton, Alberta T5J 4L6

Fig. 6. continued.

ALBERTA PROVINCIAL NOMINEE PROGRAM

FOR OFFICE USE ONLY
Employer File Number:

Applicant File Number:

NOC:

Guaranteed Job Offer

Guaranteed Job Offer Form ABPNP 002

Employer Requirements:

An employer's application to have a skilled worker nominated for immigration under the Alberta Provincial Nominee Program will be considered if the employment offer:

- Is for permanent, full-time position(s) in Alberta;
- Meets provincial employment and wage standards;
- Is made to an individual who meets the required qualifications for the position; and
- Does not conflict with existing collective bargaining agreements

Please note:

This application must be completed in full with accompanying attachments, failure to comply will result in a delay in processing.

A. Employer Information:

Employer File Number:

Employer Name: Name of Employer Contact:

Telephone: Facsimile: E-mail: Website:

Mailing Address: City/Town: Postal Code:

B. Prospective Employee Information:

Employee Family Name: Given Name:

Mailing address: Address of residence (complete if mailing address is a post office box or different from place of residence):

Telephone number: Facsimile number: E-mail address:

Does the employee have a **Temporary Foreign Worker** Authorization:

☐ YES   ☐ NO   If yes, please attach supporting documents

Alberta
GOVERNMENT OF ALBERTA
CANADA

ABPNP 002 (03/2002)   1

Fig. 7.   Guaranteed job offer form.

**ALBERTA PROVINCIAL
NOMINEE PROGRAM**

C. Position Information:

1. Occupation:

2. Position Description:
   Please attach detailed description and required qualifications

3. Is this a permanent and full-time position:
   ☐ YES   ☐ NO

4. Salary:

5. Address of employment:

6. Education requirements:
   ☐ University   ☐ Trade school/college
   ☐ Other (please specify): _____

7. Canadian/Alberta industry/association standards required:
   ☐ Association standards   ☐ Industry standards
   ☐ Journeyman standards   ☐ Other: _____

8. Union: ☐ YES   ☐ NO
   If yes, please specify:

   _____

9. Language fluency required for position:

English:	Read	Speak	Write	French:	Read	Speak	Write
Fluent:	☐	☐	☐	Fluent:	☐	☐	☐
Well:	☐	☐	☐	Well:	☐	☐	☐
Functional:	☐	☐	☐	Functional:	☐	☐	☐

10. Recruitment Activity:

(a) How did you learn about this employee? (Please check all boxes that apply)
   ☐ Employer Recruiting Activities   ☐ Industry Association
   ☐ Employee initiated contact with employer   ☐ Immigration consultant
   ☐ Other (please specify): _____

(b) Did you contact any of Alberta's Economic Development's international offices? If so, please note which one(s):

_____

Please attach copy of contract between your company and the employee, which includes signatures of your authorized signing officer, and employee accepting the offer and conditions of employment.

D. Authorization:

I certify that the information provided for this application is true and correct. I certify that to my knowledge, the offer of employment does not conflict with any existing bargaining agreements, the settlement of any labour dispute or the employment of a person involved in such a dispute. I understand that the information in this form may be used for purposes of evaluating the Alberta Provincial Nominee Program, and I affirm that the employer named above agrees to be contacted in the future for purposes of evaluating the Alberta Provincial Nominee Program.

If this application form and material has been completed by my Agent, on my behalf, I authorize my Agent to provide the completed form and material to the Alberta Government. I further authorize my Agent and the Alberta Government to discuss the content of my application, or additional information of this type, for the purposes described in this form.

Name of Authorized Signing Officer: (please print)

Title of Authorized Signing Officer:

Signature of Authorized Signing Officer:

Date Signed: (dd/mm/yyyy)

Fig. 7. continued.

ALBERTA PROVINCIAL
NOMINEE PROGRAM

The personal information that you provide on this form is collected under the authority of Section 8 of the *Government Organization Act* (RSA 2000) and Section 33(a) and (c) of the *Freedom of Information and Protection of Privacy Act* (RSA 2000). The information will be used to contact you regarding your company's application under the Alberta Provincial Nominee Program. If you have any questions about the collection of this information you can contact the Provincial Nominee Program (PNP), Alberta Economic Development, 4th Floor, Commerce Place, 10155 – 102 Street, Edmonton, Alberta Canada T5J 4L6. Telephone: (780) 427-6764; Facsimile: (780) 427-6560.

If a person other than the applicant has prepared this form, please complete the following:
This form has been prepared by:

☐ lawyer   Name: _____
                     Address: _____

☐ immigration consultant   _____
                     Telephone: _____

☐ other:_____   E-mail: _____

CHECKLIST:

The following documentation is required by the Alberta Provincial Nominee Program in order to process your application:

☐ Completed application form Guaranteed Job Offer (ABPNP 002)
☐ Detailed position description and required qualifications
☐ Contract between employer and prospective employee

If candidate is a Temporary foreign worker the following copies of documents are required:

☐ validation letter to the employer from Human Resource Development Canada (HRDC)
☐ EMPLOYMENT AUTHORIZATION from Citizenship and Immigration Canada (CIC)

Send completed application form and accompanying attachments to:

Alberta Provincial Nominee Program
Alberta Economic Development
4th Floor, 10155 — 102 Street
Edmonton, Alberta T5J 4L6

Fig. 7. continued.

**ALBERTA PROVINCIAL
NOMINEE PROGRAM**

FOR OFFICE USE ONLY
Applicant File Number:
Employer File Number:
NOC:

Skilled Worker/Professional

Skilled Worker/Professional ABPNP 003

DO NOT SUBMIT THIS APPLICATION UNLESS YOU HAVE A JOB OFFER FROM A PRE-APPROVED EMPLOYER

The personal information that you provide in your application forms and supporting materials is collected under the authority of Section 8 of the *Government Organization Act* (RSA 2000) and Section 33(a) and (c) of the *Freedom of Information and Protection of Privacy Act* (RSA 2000). The information will be used to assist in evaluating your suitability for the Alberta Provincial Nominee Program and for follow-up if you are admitted into Canada. If you have any questions about the collection of this information you can contact the Provincial Nominee Program (PNP), Alberta Economic Development, 4th Floor, Commerce Place, 10155 — 102 Street, Edmonton, Alberta Canada T5J 4L6. Telephone: (780) 427-6764; Facsimile: (780) 427-6560.

ALL POTENTIAL IMMIGRANTS AGE 18 OR OLDER MUST COMPLETE THE CITIZENSHIP AND IMMIGRATION CANADA FORMS (IMM0008 AND IMM5406, if applicable) AND SUBMIT WITH THIS APPLICATION.

PLEASE PRINT OR TYPE APPLICATION

A. Contact Information:

1. I am: ☐ The Applicant ☐ A Consultant ☐ A Lawyer ☐ Other _____

2. Has the applicant or a family member accompanying the applicant previously been approved or made for admission to Canada as an immigrant.

☐ Yes ☐ No

If yes, please provide:

Immigration office contacted: _____

Citizenship and Immigration Canada (CIC) File Number: _____

Date(s) of application: _____

Status: _____

Name(s) of applicant: _____

Category of Application(s): ☐ Independent Class ☐ Entrepreneur ☐ Self-Employed

☐ Family Class ☐ PNP ☐ Other: _____

Province of application: _____

B. Personal Information:

1. a) Surname (family name): b) Given name(s):

2. a) Date of birth (day/month/year): b) Place of birth (city or town): c) Country of birth:

GOVERNMENT OF ALBERTA
CANADA

ABPNP003 (09/2003)
This form is made available by the Alberta Provincial Government and is not to be sold to applicants.

1

Fig. 8.   Sample skilled worker form.

**ALBERTA PROVINCIAL
NOMINEE PROGRAM**

3. Gender: ☐ Male ☐ Female   4. Citizenship: 5. Country of residence:

6. a) Mailing address: b) Address of residence (complete if mailing address is a post office box or different from place of residence):

c) Telephone number: d) Facsimile number: e) E-mail address:

C. Occupation and Education

1. a) Current occupation: b) Intended occupation in Alberta: _____

                                            Do you have an offer of employment:
                                            ☐ Yes ☐ No
                                            If yes, please specify employer name: _____

2. Education history (provide supporting certified documents, certificates, diplomas —use separate sheet, if required):
(a) Total years of education: _____
(b) Level of Education:

☐ Less than Secondary   ☐ Secondary completed   ☐ Some post-graduate studies but no degree
☐ Formal Trade certificate/apprenticeship ☐ Some university, but no degree ☐ Non-university certificate or diploma
☐ Bachelors degree   ☐ Masters degree   ☐ PhD

3. Work history — list all employment since age 18 (use a separate sheet if required) and attach supporting documentation:
   a)   Total years of employment: _____

Date (from/to)	Name of Employer	City/Country	Occupation	Gross Salary

4. Language: Fluent in English   Fluent in French   Native Language:

                 Speak ☐ Yes ☐ No   Speak ☐ Yes ☐ No   _____
                 Read   ☐ Yes ☐ No   Read   ☐ Yes ☐ No
                 Write ☐ Yes ☐ No   Write ☐ Yes ☐ No   What other languages do you speak?

                                                                    _____

Fig. 8. continued.

**ALBERTA PROVINCIAL
NOMINEE PROGRAM**

D. Dependents and Family

1. List those who will accompany the applicant to Canada and also include dependents that are Canadian citizens or permanent residents (use separate sheet if required):

	Spouse	Dependant 1	Dependant 2	Dependant 3
Family Name (Surname)	_____	_____	_____	_____
Given Name(s)	_____	_____	_____	_____
Gender	☐ Male ☐ Female	☐ Male ☐ Female	☐ Male ☐ Female	☐ Male ☐ Female
Date of birth	_____ (dd/mm/yyyy)	_____ (dd/mm/yyyy)	_____ (dd/mm/yyyy)	_____ (dd/mm/yyyy)

2. Spouse:
Occupation: _____

Indicate level of education:

☐ Less than Secondary
☐ Formal Trade certificate/apprenticeship
☐ Bachelors degree

☐ Secondary completed
☐ Some university, but no degree
☐ Masters degree

☐ Some post-graduate studies but no degree
☐ Non-university certificate or diploma
☐ PhD

3. List relatives in Canadian Provinces/Territories of applicant/spouse (use attachment if additional space required)

Name of Relative	Relationship to applicant or spouse	Town/City & Province of Relative	Years in Canada
_____	_____	_____	_____
_____	_____	_____	_____
_____	_____	_____	_____
_____	_____	_____	_____

4. Please list any visits you have made to Canada (use attachment if additional space required):

Reason for Visit	Province	Length of Stay	Year of Visit
_____	_____	_____	_____
_____	_____	_____	_____
_____	_____	_____	_____
_____	_____	_____	_____
_____	_____	_____	_____

5. Assistance in completing application:

Did you have help preparing your PNP immigration form: ☐ Yes ☐ No

If yes, who provided this assistance: ☐ employer ☐ immigration consultant ☐ lawyer ☐ other (please specify):

ABPNP003 (09/2003)
This form is made available by the Alberta Provincial Government and is not to be sold to applicants.

Fig. 8. continued.

**ALBERTA PROVINCIAL
NOMINEE PROGRAM**

6. How did you learn about the Alberta Provincial Nominee Program (you may check more than one box):

☐ Employer   ☐ AB Promotion Materials   ☐ PNP Website
☐ Visa office   ☐ Other: _____

Applicant's Statements and Authorization

Statements

1. I confirm that the information I have given in this application is truthful, complete and correct and has personally been provided by me.

2. I understand that any false statements or concealment of information may result in the Alberta Government refusing my application or, if applicable, my nomination.

3. I understand all the above information, having asked for and obtained an explanation of every point which was unclear to me.

Authorization to Collect and Disclose Personal Information to Process My Immigration Application

4. I authorize the Alberta Government to disclose, as necessary, any personal information provided to or collected by the Alberta Government with respect to my application under the Provincial Nominee Program, to officials administering immigration programs within the Government of Canada.

5. I authorize the Government of Canada to disclose, as necessary, personal information about me collected under the Immigration Act and Regulations to the officials administering immigration programs within the Alberta Government, and authorize the Alberta Government to collect such information.

6. If these application forms and material have been completed by my Agent, on my behalf, I authorize my Agent to provide the completed forms and material to the Alberta Government. I further authorize my Agent and the Alberta Government to discuss the contents of my application, or additional information of this type, for the purposes described in this form.

7. I authorize the Alberta Government to contact any individuals or businesses that I have referenced in my application forms and material, as necessary, to verify the information I have provided or to seek additional related information from them.

8. I authorize the Alberta Government to disclose to my future Alberta employer information regarding the status of my immigration application, from time to time, throughout the process.

9. I authorize my future Alberta employer to provide details of our contract of employment to the Alberta Government, and authorize the Alberta Government to collect such information.

Date: _____

Applicant name: _____   _____
                        (please print)   (signature)

if applicable:
Spouse name: _____   _____
                        (please print)   (signature)

Fig. 8. continued.

**ALBERTA PROVINCIAL
NOMINEE PROGRAM**

If a person other than the applicant has prepared this form, please complete the following:

This form has been prepared by:

☐ lawyer

☐ immigration consultant

☐ other:_____

Name: _____

Address: _____

_____

Telephone: _____

E-mail: _____

CHECKLIST:

The following documentation is required by the Alberta Provincial Nominee Program in order to process your application:

☐ Completed application form Skilled Worker/Professional (ABPNP 003)
☐ Completed IMM008
☐ Completed IMM5406 —if applicable
☐ Applicant's and Spouse's certified documents supporting education history (certificates, diplomas, degrees)
☐ Applicant's and Spouse's documents supporting work history (reference letters, work permits)
☐ Copies of passports for applicant and dependents

Send completed application form and accompanying attachments to:

Alberta Provincial Nominee Program
Alberta Economic Development
4th Floor, 10155 — 102 Street
Edmonton, Alberta T5J 4L6
Canada

ABPNP003 (09/2003)
This form is made available by the Alberta Provincial Government and is not to be sold to applicants.

5

Fig. 8. continued.

5:3 THE BRITISH COLUMBIA PNP

The British Columbia PNP is divided into the following categories: Strategic Occupations, Business Skills and Projects.

5:3.1 Strategic Occupations category

An important aspect of this category of the programme is the fact that it is not run by a specific skill shortage *list* (like the Manitoba PNP, which is described in more detail below). Rather, the province will assess applications on a case-by-case basis, focusing on the following aspects:

◆ the existing shortages of qualified workers at a particular time; and

◆ the level of skill involved (i.e. the skill level of the job must be high).

5:3.1.a Shortages

Currently, the province has identified certain sectors as high priorities: aerospace, post-secondary education, information and high technology. However, if employers in other industries identify key shortages and can prove them with required documentation, they can also apply.

5:3.1.b The level of skill

Individuals considered for nomination will generally have considerable education and experience, and often will be developing or using new knowledge, skills or technologies. In many cases, these individuals will bring new skills to the provincial workforce.

An employer should not apply under the PNP for approval if the position offered falls under one of the categories listed below:

◆ medium and lower level management;

◆ most administration and all clerical occupations;

◆ retail sales, both management and salespersons;

◆ most hospitality industry jobs and other service sector jobs where training periods are short;

◆ semi-skilled manufacturing and fabricating jobs;

◆ helpers and unskilled labour in construction, agriculture and resource industries.

This is not an exhaustive list. Other fields for which shortages are unlikely to be seen as requiring recruitment of foreign workers include recreation supervisors, employment and family counsellors, editors and journalists, lawyers, general accountants and bookkeepers, civil engineers and technicians, forestry technicians, draftspersons, bicycle repairers, small engine repairers, tailors, roofers and floor covering installers.

Apart from shortage and the high level of the skill, the other factors considered are the ones mentioned above in section 5:1.1.a.

For a list of documents to be submitted in a Strategic Occupations application, please see Figure 9. For more information about the Strategic Occupations category, visit **www.mcaws.gov.bc.ca/amip/pnp/** and contact:

Province of
British Columbia
Ministry of Community,
Aboriginal and Women's Services

BRITISH
COLUMBIA

PNP Strategic Occupations Checklist

British Columbia Provincial Nominee Program (BC PNP)

The checklist below provides **requirements for a complete Strategic Occupations application for the British Columbia Provincial Nominee Program (BC PNP).** Please complete this checklist and submit it with your application to the BC PNP. If you cannot obtain any required items, please provide a written explanation. If you are a nurse, you should obtain the checklist specific to nurses through Health Match BC. Please note, the BC PNP reserves the right to ask for additional items if it deems such a request necessary.

REQUIRED DOCUMENTS FOR A COMPLETE STRATEGIC OCCUPATIONS APPLICATION

---

1. BC PROVINCIAL NOMINEE PROGRAM (BC PNP) FORMS

- ❏ **GUARANTEED JOB OFFER FORM** (to be filled out by the employer)
- ❏ **INFORMATION RELEASE FORM** (to be filled out by the applicant and spouse)
- ❏ **NOMINEE INFORMATION FORM** (to be filled out by the applicant)

---

2. EMPLOYMENT INFORMATION

- ❏ **RECOMMENDATION LETTER FROM THE EMPLOYER**
  Ensure that this letter specifically states that the employer **recommends** the applicant for nomination under the BC PNP. The letter should explain how the employer found out about the applicant, why (s)he is suitable for the position, and how (s)he is likely to contribute to the future success of the company.

- ❏ **DETAILED JOB DESCRIPTION**
  Outline all of the specific duties of the position. For information technology positions, describe the specific **technical** skills required for the position and the types of projects the position would be responsible for.

- ❏ **JOB OFFER**
  Ensure that the job offer is signed by the employer and includes a statement of acceptance **signed** by the applicant. The offer should outline the terms of employment, such as the salary level and hours of work.

- ❏ **COMPANY INFORMATION**
  Include information on the employing company, such as company brochures, website printouts, or a photocopy of the certificate of incorporation.

- ❏ **RESUME AND EDUCATION CERTIFICATES**
  Include the applicant's resume and photocopies of any education, trade, or course certificates that are relevant to the position offered.

FOR APPLICANTS WHO WILL BE WORKING IN A FIELD THAT HAS MANDATORY REGULATORY/LICENSING REQUIREMENTS:

- ❏ **PROOF THAT LICENSING/REGULATORY REQUIREMENTS HAVE BEEN MET**
  Provide a photocopy of a permit, registration card, or a letter of approval from the regulatory body.

FOR APPLICANTS (AND THEIR DEPENDENTS) <u>WHO ARE CURRENLTY RESIDING IN CANADA</u>:

- ❏ **WORK PERMIT**
  Submit a photocopy only.

  OR

- ❏ **ANOTHER DOCUMENT CONFERRING STATUS IN CANADA**
  Submit a photocopy of a temporary resident visa, a study permit, or a stamp in a passport.

Fig. 9.   List of documents for strategic occupations application.

Province of British Columbia Ministry of Community, Aboriginal and Women's Services	**PNP Strategic Occupations Checklist**
	British Columbia Provincial Nominee Program (BC PNP)

---

3. EVIDENCE OF SKILL SHORTAGES

❏ **WRITTEN STATEMENT FROM THE EMPLOYER:**
- describing any attempts to recruit or train Canadians for the position, such as placing job advertisements, attending job fairs, hiring a recruitment agent, or initiating in-house training;
- explaining why the Canadians who applied for the position were not hired; and
- explaining why any employees were laid off in the last two years, if applicable.

❏ **PROOF OF RECRUITMENT EFFORTS**
Provide proof of attempts to hire Canadian Citizens or Permanent Residents, such as photocopies of bills for recruitment activities, or photocopies or printouts of job advertisements.

❏ **SKILL SHORTAGE EVIDENCE**
If available, provide evidence of skill shortages in the industry, such as industry reports.

---

4. CITIZENSHIP AND IMMIGRATION CANADA (CIC) FORMS

Applicant	Spouse/Partner	Dependent Child 18+	
❏	❏	❏	**Schedule 1:** Background/Declaration
❏	❏	❏	**Additional Family Information:** IMM5406
❏			**IMM008:** Application for Permanent Residence in Canada
❏			**Schedule 4:** Economic Classes - Provincial Nominee
❏			**Appendix A** Checklist

Only **send photocopies of CIC forms** to the BC PNP. Any **spouse/partner** or **dependent child who is 18 or over** must complete a separate *Schedule 1: Background/Declaration* and *IMM5406: Additional Family Information* form, whether or not (s)he plans to accompany the applicant to Canada.

The **Appendix A Checklist** outlines the materials required for a permanent residence application to CIC. BC PNP applicants should check off the items on the checklist that they have already obtained. Applicants **do not** need to submit the actual materials indicated on the checklist (other than the CIC forms) to the BC PNP.

Fig. 9. continued.

Province of
British Columbia
Ministry of Community,
Aboriginal and Women's Services

PNP Strategic Occupations Checklist

British Columbia Provincial Nominee Program (BC PNP)

---

5. CONSENT TO DISCLOSE INFORMATION TO A REPRESENTATIVE

These items are only **for applicants and employers who are represented by an immigration lawyer or consultant.** The BC PNP requires permission from the applicant and employer to disclose information to the representative about the application. **Please Note:** individuals **do not** need to hire a representative in order to submit an application to the BC PNP or to CIC.

❑   **CONSENT FROM THE APPLICANT (EMPLOYEE)**
The BC PNP needs written permission from the applicant to disclose information about the BC PNP application to a representative. Applicants can use the standardized form : *Letter of Authorization for Release of Information to a Third Party: Employee.*

❑   **CONSENT FROM THE EMPLOYER**
The BC PNP needs written permission from the employer to disclose information about the BC PNP application to a representative. Employers can use the standardized form: *Letter of Authorization for Release of Information to a Third Party: Employer.*

Standardized consent forms can be found on the BC PNP website at www.mcaws.gov.bc.ca/amip/pnp under "Application Forms"

If you have questions about BC PNP requirements, you may contact us by telephone (250-387-6540) or by e-mail (PNPinfo@Victoria1.gov.bc.ca).

You may **submit completed applications to the BC PNP by fax, mail, or courier at the following number/addresses**

Fax: 250-387-3725

Mail: British Columbia Provincial Nominee Program
              Immigration Division
              Ministry of Community, Aboriginal and Women's Services
              PO Box 9214 Stn Prov Govt
              Victoria BC V8W 9J1

Courier: British Columbia Provincial Nominee Program
              Immigration Division
              Ministry of Community, Aboriginal and Women's Services
              Second Floor
              800 Johnson Street
              Victoria BC V8W 9N7

If you are submitting applications by mail or courier, do NOT put material in binders or protective plastic covers.

Fig. 9. continued.

The Ministry of Community, Aboriginal and Women's
  Services
Immigration Branch
Provincial Nominee Program
P.O. Box 9214 Stn. Prov. Gov't
Victoria BC V8W 9J1
Canada
Tel: (250) 387-6540
Fax: (250) 387-3725
E-mail: **PNPinfo@Victoria1.gov.bc.ca**

With regard to the British Columbia PNP, it should be noted
that **registered nurses are, at the time of preparation of these
materials, in high demand in the province.** As such there
is an expedited procedure for such applicants under the
programme. For information specific to this issue, please
visit **www.mcaws.gov.bc.ca/amip/pnp/** and contact:

Tara McAteer
Search Analyst
Health Match BC
Suite 200–1333 W. Broadway
Vancouver BC V6H 4C6
Canada
Tel: (604) 736-5920 Ext 222
Fax: (604) 736-5963
E-mail: **tarac@healthmatchbc.org**
Web site: **www.healthmatchbc.org**

5:3.2 Business Skills category

This category allows people with extensive resources and
business experience to apply for permanent residence in

British Columbia, provided that they satisfy the following eligibility criteria:

◆ successful business experience;

◆ minimum net worth of CDN$ 2 million;

◆ minimum investment in the business of CDN$ 1 million;

◆ applicant to own at least $1/3$ of the equity in the business;

◆ a business plan;

◆ business to create a minimum of five new jobs;

◆ applicant to have an active management role.

For more information, please contact:

Ministry of Competition, Science and Enterprise
BC Trade and Investment Office
999 Canada Place
Vancouver BC V8C 3E1
Canada
Tel: (604) 844-1810
Fax: (604) 660-4092
E-mail: **Bus.imm@gems7.gov.bc.ca**
Web site: **www.cse.gov.bc.ca/subwebs/busimm/
app-process.htm**

5:3.3 Projects category

This category is designed to assist companies with the timely entry of skilled key managers and key technical professionals essential to the success of a business expected to generate significant economic benefits to the province. The eligibility criteria are as follows:

◆ the company must have a proven record of successful experience in an area relevant to the proposed business;

◆ the position relates to new investments or business expansions (minimum CDN$1 million);

◆ key staff presence is essential to the success of the province.

For more information, please contact:

Ministry of Competition, Science and Enterprise
BC Trade and Investment Office
999 Canada Place
Vancouver BC V8C 3E1
Canada
Tel: (604) 844-1810
Fax: (604) 660-4092
E-mail: **Bus.imm@gems7.gov.bc.ca**
Web site: **www.cse.gov.bc.ca/subwebs/busimm/**
   app-process.htm

5:4 THE MANITOBA PNP

The Manitoba PNP is divided into the following categories: Skilled Workers and Business Immigrants.

5:4.1 Skilled Workers

If you are a skilled worker and you are interested in living and working in Manitoba, you can apply to the provincial authorities yourself. Your application will be accepted for consideration only if you can demonstrate proof of one or more of the following:

- you have past education or work experience in Manitoba;

- you have a guaranteed job offer consistent with your training and experience;

- you have family or community support in Manitoba to assist you upon your arrival in the province.

In Manitoba, you have the best chance of being nominated if your training and work experience is in demand. The province has an overall demand for skilled workers and professionals in a number of specific industrial and economic sectors. Please see Figure 10 for the Manitoba High Demand Occupation List and the required sets of conditions associated with each listed occupation.

You can download a Self-Assessment Guide online at **www.gov.mb.ca/labour/immigrate/immigration/2.html**. For the complete checklist of documents and information to be included in your nomination application, please see Figure 11.

5:4.2 Business Immigrants

The eligibility criteria under this category of the Manitoba PNP are the following:

- minimum personal net worth of CDN$250,000;

- minimum amount of equity investment in Manitoba of CDN$150,000;

MANITOBA PROVINCIAL NOMINEE PROGRAM
HIGH DEMAND OCCUPATIONS LIST
(HDOL-MB PNP) Effective December 18, 2001

A. The following occupations will only be assessed (15 points) under occupational demand selection criteria if the applicant is able to provide the required documentation (education and experience) and has the minimum years of related experience.

Occupation	Specific Skills, Comments or Documents Required (all require proof of appropriate training)	Minimum Years Experience
Bricklayer	Must be journeyperson or have equivalent from own country	3 years
*Cabinetmaker		3 years
*Heavy-duty Equipment Mechanic	Documented computer/electronic skills	3 years
*Long Haul Truck Driver	Documented air brake endorsement from employer, clean driving record	2 years
Machining Tool Operator	Documented CNC experience	3 years
Machinist	Documented CNC experience	3 years
*Motor Vehicle Body Repairer		3 years
*Motor Vehicle Mechanic	Documented computer/electronic skills and work with airbags	3 years
Sheet Metal Worker	3 years experience must be in composite and sheet metal repair in aircraft maintenance	3 years
Tool & Die Maker		3 years
Welder		3 years
Pattern maker in Garment Manufacturing		1 year
Industrial Instrument Technician	1 year experience must be in plastics manufacturing	1 year
Nondestructive Tester and Inspector		3 years
Electrical & Electronics Engineer	Professional designation from own country	3 years
Electrical & Electronic Engineering Technologist and Technician	Professional designation from own country	3 years
Industrial Engineering and Manufacturing Technologist and Technician	Professional designation from own country	3 years
Industrial and Manufacturing Engineer	Professional designation from own country	3 years
Computer Programmer	3 years experience must be in area(s) described Visual Basic, C, Java, C++ combined with data base design and systems analysis skills	3 years
Computer Engineer	Professional designation from own country	5 years
Information Systems Business Analyst and Consultant	Must show e-commerce experience and fluency in English or French	3 years
Software Engineer		3 years
Web Designer/Graphic Illustrator		3 years
*Aircraft Assembler & Inspector	Valid trade license from own country; 3 years experience with commercial airlines	3 years
*Aircraft Maintenance Engineer	Valid trade license from own country; 3 years experience with commercial airlines	3 years
*Aircraft Maintenance Technician	Valid trade license from own country; 3 years experience with commercial airlines	3 years

1 of 2

Fig. 10.   Manitoba high demand occupation list.

Note that applicants approved under these occupations may be able to work in jobs related to their training and experience, however may not be recognized in status or pay until necessary steps are taken to receive license, accreditation, registration papers or other documents that may be required. While these applications will be assessed under MB PNP, applicants are strongly encouraged to consider licensing or accreditation issues before applying.

B. **The following occupations will only be assessed (15 points) under the occupational demand selection criteria if there is a guaranteed job offer from a Manitoba employer. Guaranteed job offer and applicant must meet conditions set out in Factor 4 Guaranteed Employment.**

Occupation	Minimum Years Experience
Chef	As identified by employer
College & Other Vocational Instructor	As identified by employer
Construction Contractor/Manager	5 years
Financial Auditors and Accountant	3 years
Hog Barn Manager	3 years
Information Systems & Data Processing Manager	As identified by employer
Marketing & Advertising Manager: fluent in English or French	5 years
Pork Production Technician	1 year
Psychologist	As identified by employer
Social and Community Services Worker and Family Counsellor	As identified by employer
Technical Sales Specialist	As identified by employer
University Professor	As identified by employer

C. **Industry Initiatives.** Employers and/or industries may be experiencing unique shortages of skilled workers in occupations not represented above and/or in numbers that require coordinated recruitment efforts. Employers will be asked to outline vacant positions, shortages and recruitment plans. Mutually agreed upon terms will result in Industry Initiatives where applicants not listed above can receive 15 points under the MB PNP.

D. **Licensed Occupations.** In addition to the above, the Government of Manitoba recognizes that there are documented shortages in a number of other occupations that require licensing in order to work in Manitoba. Manitoba Labour and Immigration reserves the right to require valid license to practice in these occupations before assessment and/or approval under PN. The list includes: *specialist physicians, general practitioners, optometrists, veterinarians, physiotherapists, occupational therapists, registered nurses, registered psychiatric nurses, medical radiation technicians, pharmacists, secondary school teachers, rehabilitation/special needs teachers and early childhood educators.* Applications for persons working in these occupations will be considered on the HDOL when the applicant is able to provide proof of being licensed and has a guaranteed job offer from a Manitoba employer at the time of submitting the Provincial Nominee application.

NOTE: Applications will be considered from skilled foreign temporary workers currently working in Manitoba whose occupation is not represented above. Human Resources Development Canada must have validated the current position and the employment authorization must be valid and eligible for extension if required. Current employer may be contacted to determine the need for permanent workers in that occupation and/or willingness to hire on a permanent basis.

Fig. 10. continued.

Document Checklist

READ THIS CAREFULLY AND INCLUDE ALL REQUIRED DOCUMENTS WHEN SUBMITTING YOUR APPLICATION. Translations are required for any documents in languages other than English or French. The translation must be directly attached to a copy of the original document.

Assemble your documents in the order listed below. Attach the necessary DOCUMENT CHECKLIST TAGS provided in this package. Use this checklist to make sure that you have all the required documents. Do not submit your application until it is complete.

	DOCUMENT	✓ or n/a (not applicable)	
		Principal Applicant	Dependent (s)
1.	**APPLICATION FOR PERMANENT RESIDENCE IN CANADA FORM (IMM 0008-Generic)** – 2 pages		
	Completed and signed form IMM 0008-Generic from principal applicant and each family member 18 years of age or over..	☐	☐
	Photocopy of one current passport-size photograph for each member of your family. Do not send originals. Original photographs will be needed later for CIC.	☐	☐

Fig. 11.   Sample document checklist
(Manitoba PNP – Skilled Workers Application).

	DOCUMENT	✓ or n/a (not applicable)	
		Principal Applicant	Dependent (s)
2.	**BACKGROUNDER/DECLARATION FORM (IMM 0008-Schedule 1)** –4 pages Completed and signed form IMM 0008-Generic from principal applicant, spouse or common-law partner and each dependent child 18 years of age or over, whether they are accompanying you to Canada or not.	☐	☐
	Previous refusal letter(s) or other correspondence from CIC and/or Provincial Nominee Programs.	☐	☐
3.	**ADDITIONAL FAMILY INFORMATION FORM (IMM 5406)** - 1 page Completed and signed form IMM 5406 from principal applicant, spouse or common-law partner and each dependent child 18 years of age or over, whether they are accompanying you to Canada or not.	☐	☐
4.	**ECONOMIC CLASSES-PROVINCIAL NOMINEES FORM (IMM 0008-Schedule 4)** – 1 page Completed and signed form IMM 0008-Schedule 4 from principal applicant and any adult accompanying children.	☐	☐
5.	**MANITOBA SUPPLEMENTARY INFORMATION FORM (MSUP)** – 4 pages Only ONE MSUP form to be completed by principal applicant although some questions require answers by spouse. Check that the appropriate questions are answered in full and the form is signed by both principal applicant and spouse, if married. Spouse must sign even if not accompanying you to Canada.	☐	☐
6.	**INFORMATION RELEASE FORM (MREL)** – 1 page Completed and signed by principal applicant and spouse, dated and witnessed.	☐	☐
7.	**RELEASE OF INFORMATION FOR EVALUATION OF PNP (MEVA)** – 1 page Completed, signed by principal applicant and spouse, dated and witnessed.	☐	☐
8.	**AUTHORITY TO RELEASE INFORMATION TO DESIGNATED INDIVIDUALS FORM (IMM 5476)** – 1 page Completed and signed signed by principal applicant and each family member 18 years of age or older.	☐	☐
9.	**IMMIGRATION REPRESENTATIVES** Code of Conduct for Immigration Representatives (MCC JAN 2003) signed by principal applicant	☐	☐
	Code signed by immigration representative	☐	☐
	Proof of Canadian citizenship or Permanent Resident status	☐	☐

Fig. 11. continued.

	DOCUMENT	✓ or n/a (not applicable)	
		Principal Applicant	Dependent (s)
10.	**IDENTITY / MARRIAGE INFORMATION** Birth certificates, for both you and your spouse, showing names of parents. If applicable, also provide:		
	• Marriage certificate	☐	☐
	• Death certificate	☐	☐
	• Divorce certificate or proof of separation	☐	☐
	• National Identity Card/Certificate or Cedula	☐	☐
	(If the information differs on any of these documents, provide a sworn affidavit explaining the differences.)		
	If divorced or separated and you have children under the age of 18 provide:		
	• Custody agreement for children under the age of 18.	☐	☐
	• If children are accompanying you, provide proof that they may do so. This could include a letter from former spouse supporting your move. If children are not accompanying you, prove that you have fulfilled any obligations stated in custody agreement. This could include a letter from spouse giving permission for PA to move from the country.	☐	☐
11.	**CHILDREN'S INFORMATION** Birth certificate for each child showing parentage (naming both parents). Adoption papers	☐	☐
	If dependent children are 22 years of age or older, submit proof of continuous full time studies. Provide letter(s) from the school(s), signed by a school official, confirming continued enrolment in full time studies since turning 22 years of age.	☐	☐
12.	**PASSPORT / TRAVEL DOCUMENTS** Copies of passport or travel documents that are valid for at least two years for yourself, your spouse and dependent children. Submit copies of pages showing the passport number, date of issue and expiration, your photo, name, date and place of birth, as well as occupation, if applicable.	☐	☐
	If you live in a country other than your country of citizenship, include a copy of your visa for the country in which you currently live.	☐	☐
	Include copies of entry visas or Immigration stamps in your passport from previous visits to Canada.	☐	☐
13.	**EDUCATION INFORMATION** Educational degrees, diplomas or certificates, and professional licences, for both the principal applicant and spouse.	☐	☐
	Official transcripts showing school(s) attended, courses taken and duration of program, must also be included.	☐	☐
	All documents must be translated into English or French.	☐	☐
14.	**EVIDENCE OF LANGUAGE ABILITY IN ENGLISH AND/OR FRENCH** Proof of your ability in English or French as demonstrated or explained by you in Factor 7 (self-assessment guide)	☐	☐

Fig. 11. continued.

	DOCUMENT	✓ or n/a (not applicable)	
		Principal Applicant	Dependent (s)
15.	**EMPLOYMENT INFORMATION** Copies of letters of reference detailing both the principal applicant and spouse's work experience for the past 10 years, including present employment. Each letter must include: • specific period of employment with the company (start and end dates). • position(s) held, and time spent in each position. • list of tasks/duties and main responsibilities in each position. • letter must be on company letterhead and signed by an authorized representative of the company, including their name and title. Copy of a résumé summarizing your work history and education and training.	☐ ☐	☐ ☐
16.	**EMPLOYMENT OFFER** • Offer of employment on company letterhead to include job title, job description and salary. • Semi-skilled applicants who are presently working in Manitoba under a Work Permit and meet MPNP criteria for that category may be eligible for points in the High Demand Occupation Factor. Applicants must submit a valid Work Permit visa and an offer of permanent employment from a Manitoba-based employer that has been designated by MPNP. • Do NOT submit a completed MPNP Guaranteed Employment Offer form with your application. Manitoba Labour and Immigration will contact the employer directly to complete the form whether or not one has been submitted with the application.	☐ ☐	☐ ☐
17.	**REGIONAL DEVELOPMENT** Proof of your ties to a rural or northern region of Manitoba. See Factor 5: Regional Development (self-assessment guide).	☐	☐
18.	**PROOF OF RELATIONSHIP TO FAMILY IN MANITOBA** Birth certificates (showing parents' names) of the relatives through whom you trace your roots AND Relative's Canadian Passport, Certificate of Citizenship, Record of Landing (IMM 1000), Confirmation of Permanent Record (IMM 5292) or Permanent resident card AND Manitoba Health Card	☐ ☐ ☐	☐ ☐ ☐
19.	**FAMILY-LIKE SUPPORT** **Originals** of the Summary and individual Affidavits must be submitted. • Notarized Affidavits of Family-Like Support signed by five adults (summary and individual forms available from Manitoba Labour and Immigration), AND • Canadian Citizenship certificate, Canadian birth certificate, Record of Landing (IMM 1000), Confirmation of Permanent Residence (IMM 5292) or Permanent resident card for each of the five adults, AND • • Manitoba Health Card for each of the five adults.	☐ ☐ ☐	☐ ☐ ☐
20.	**EVIDENCE OF EDUCATION IN MANITOBA** Student authorization and proof of attendance from education institution	☐	☐

Fig. 11. continued.

	DOCUMENT	✓ or n/a (not applicable)	
		Principal Applicant	Dependent (s)
21.	**EVIDENCE OF WORK IN MANITOBA** Work Permit, and Letter of reference from employer.	☐ ☐	☐ ☐
22.	**SETTLEMENT FUNDS** Letters from financial institutions Bank account statements Proof of liquid assets Proof of ownership of real properties (land and buildings) AND An objective price evaluation for real properties.	☐ ☐ ☐ ☐ ☐	☐ ☐ ☐ ☐ ☐
23.	**TAGS TO ATTACH TO EACH OF THE ABOVE DOCUMENTS** Cut on the line for each number and attach to the corresponding documents	☐	☐

PUT ALL PHOTOCOPIES OF YOUR APPLICATIONS AND DOCUMENTS TOGETHER AND FORWARD THEM IN A SEALED ENVELOPE TO:

Manitoba Provincial Nominee Program
Manitoba Labour and Immigration
9th Floor – 213 Notre Dame Avenue
Winnipeg, Manitoba, R3B 1N3 CANADA

We cannot accept applications received over the internet, via electronic mail (e-mail) or by fax as forms sent in these ways often arrive incomplete, mixed and/or illegible. Your application will be reviewed and you will be contacted by letter, fax or e-mail. The program officer may request other documents to complete the assessment of your application. You will be told of the decision of the assessment in writing. Final decisions will not be given over the telephone.

If you are accepted for the Manitoba Provincial Nominee Program, you will receive a letter and further instructions about how to proceed with your application. You will need the original copy of your forms and supporting documents to comply with the instructions you will receive.

Fig. 11. continued.

◆ demonstrated business experience or extensive experience in senior management of a successful company;

◆ conducted a visit or planning a visit to Manitoba within a few months of applying to explore business opportunities and Manitoba's quality of life; and

◆ supply a cash deposit to the Government of Manitoba, in the amount of CDN$75,000 guaranteeing the establishment or purchase of a business in Manitoba. In most cases, the cash deposit will be released when the investment is made and the intended business is undertaken as outlined in your application.

You will have to submit a business proposal. For more information about the details that have to be submitted as part of the business proposal, please see Figure 12.

5:4.2.a Types of businesses that will help you become nominated

Although not an exhaustive list, value-added businesses are welcomed which provide meaningful and lasting employment in Manitoba, such as:

◆ manufacturing;

◆ food processing;

◆ ICT (information, communications and technology);

◆ primary production (mining, fishing, farming);

GUIDELINES FOR PREPARATION OF BUSINESS PROPOSALS
MANITOBA PROVINCIAL NOMINEE PROGRAM – BUSINESS

The Province of Manitoba requires that applicants under the Provincial Nominee Program for Business to provide details of the proposed business which they plan to undertake once they land in Manitoba. This business proposal is required for three reasons:

1. A sound business proposal is a good indication that the applicant has thought through the idea and has come up with a workable business to operate in Manitoba that will utilize their existing skills. The business proposal should contain a well-thought out idea; not necessarily one where all issues have been thoroughly researched, but enough to demonstrate that the business has a reasonable chance of success.

2. The Province is looking to attract those businesses which offer the greatest benefit for Manitoba. Businesses which offer more economic value for Manitoba will be favored. The types of businesses that will be given priority are: Manufacturing, Food Processing, ICT (Information Communications and Technology), Primary Production (example: mining, fishing and farming), Life Sciences (example: pharmaceuticals and biotechnology), and Energy.

3. To determine the terms and conditions of the Deposit Agreement under which the Deposit will be released.

NEW BUSINESSES
(Start-up)

For proposals involving the establishment of a new business, the applicant should provide a comprehensive outline of the business activities, with a clear indication of the following:

*   What products or services will the company be offering?
*   Who will be the customers? Will the customers be local, regional, national, or global?
*   What are the key markets?
*   How will the company market its product to these customers?
*   Where will the business be located?
*   How many and what types of jobs will be created?
*   What are the key sources of material and labor?

The applicant is also expected to produce a 2-5 year forecast, which includes an Income Statement, Balance Sheet, and accompanying notes providing details of assumptions. A great deal of guidance can be found on Industry Canada's web site at http://strategis.ic.gc.ca/cgi-bin/sc_mangb/contact_sbp/sbp_e.cgi. This provides key ratios for thousands of types of businesses in Manitoba and Canada.

19

Fig. 12.   Submitting a business proposal.

**The applicant should also provide the source/basis for their projections other than the Statistics Canada information. If the applicant's projections vary significantly from the ratios found on this web site, then this should be explained in the notes.

** Note: For applicants wishing to undertake a farming activity, please visit the website: www.gov.mb.ca/agriculture for "Farm Plan" information.

EXISTING BUSINESSES:
(Purchase of or Significant Investment in an Existing Business)

For proposals involving the purchase of or investment in an existing business, the applicant should provide a description of the current scope of the business activity, and details regarding how the applicant will change the business (if at all). The following supporting information should be provided:

1. Historic Financial Statements for at least the past 4 years (if the business has been in operation for less time, then Financial Statements since the business inception should be provided). These Financial Statements should include a Balance Sheet, Income Statement, and Statement of Changes to the Financial Position (Cash Flow);

2. Details on how many and what types of jobs will be created and/or sustained;

3. A 2-5 year forecast including Income Statement and Balance Sheet. Major changes to the business should be reflected in the forecast, and adequately explained in the notes;

4. A brief letter of intent between the existing owners and the applicant outlining the basic understanding between the two parties. This letter should not be binding and should be subject to a formal contract being entered into once the applicant has obtained their formal visa. The letter of intent should include information on:

    *   anticipated level of investment

    *   details of assets or shares to be purchased (percentage of ownership being acquired)

    *   brief details of anticipated management responsibilities

    *   if the entire business is being acquired, what, if any, will be the transitional help offered by the existing owners.

Fig. 12. continued.

◆ life sciences (pharmaceuticals and biotechnology);

◆ energy.

5:4.2.b What kind of businesses will not be considered
Although the programme offers flexibility in the types of businesses being considered, it is essential that the planned business be an operating business. Passive investments such as loan companies, property rental and investment and leasing companies will not be considered.

For more information about this category of the Manitoba PNP, please visit **www.gov.mb.ca/itm/trade/pnp-b/index.html** For more information about business in Manitoba and exploratory visits, please contact:

Manitoba Trade and Investment
1100–259 Portage Ave
Winnipeg, Manitoba, Canada R3B 3P4
Tel: (Canada 001) 204-945-2466
Fax: (Canada) 204-957-1793
E-mail: **pnp-b@gov.mb.ca**
www.manitoba-canada.com

5:5 APPLYING TO THE FEDERAL IMMIGRATION AUTHORITIES AFTER BEING NOMINATED

It is important to note that when applying to the federal immigration authorities, the Provincial Nominees are not assessed on the six selection factors that were discussed in more detail in Chapter 3. In terms of the supporting documents that must be submitted, you will have to obtain this specific information from the relevant visa office, as discussed in Chapter 1. Certainly though, include a copy of your certificate of nomination, even though the province that nominated you will send this directly to the relevant visa office. As for the processing time, once again, the relevant visa office will be in the best position to provide you with an accurate estimate of the time required.

5:6 CONTACT INFORMATION REGARDING PNPs

The following is a complete list of PNP contact information, which of course will lead to the PNP of a particular province where you may wish to settle.

Alberta

Provincial Nominee Program
Economic Immigration
Alberta Economic Development
4th Floor, Commerce Place
10155-102 Street
Edmonton, Alberta
T5J 4L6
www.alberta-canada.com/pnp

British Columbia

Provincial Nominee Program
Ministry of Community, Aboriginal and Women's Service
P.O. Box 9915 Stn. Prov. Gov't
Victoria, British Columbia
V8W 9V1
www.mcaws.gov.bc.ca/amip/pnp/

Manitoba

Provincial Nominee Program

Immigration Promotion and Recruitment Branch

Labour and Immigration Manitoba

9th Floor, 213 Notre Dame Avenue Winnipeg, Manitoba

R3B 1N3

**www.gov.mb.ca/labour/immigrate/english/
   immigration/1.html**

New Brunswick

Provincial Nominee Program

Training and Employment Development

P.O. Box 6000

Fredericton, New Brunswick

E3B 5H1

www.gnb.ca/immigration/english/index.htm

Newfoundland and Labrador

Provincial Nominee Program

Industry, Trade and Technology

Confederation Building

West Block, 4th Floor

P.O. Box 8700

St John's, Newfoundland

A1B 4J6

www.gov.nf.ca/itrd/prov_nominee.htm

Nova Scotia

Provincial Nominee Program
The Office of Economic Development
World Trade and Convention Centre
1800 Argyle Street
P.O. Box 519
Halifax, Nova Scotia
B3J 2R7
www.gov.ns.ca

Prince Edward Island

Provincial Nominee Program
Immigration and Investment Division
94 Euston Street, 2nd floor
Charlottetown, Prince Edward Island
C1A 7M8
www.gov.pe.ca

Saskatchewan

Provincial Nominee Program
Dept of Government Relations and Immigration
Immigration Branch
2nd Floor–1919 Saskatchewan Drive
Regina, Saskatchewan
S4P 3V7
www.immigrationsask.gov.sk.ca

Yukon

Provincial Nominee Program

Business Immigration, Industry Development

Business, Tourism and Culture

P.O. Box 2703

Whitehorse, Yukon

Y1A 2C6

www.economicdevelopment.gov.yk.ca

6

Permanent Residence – Business Immigration

Those who are interested in establishing themselves in Canada and who have business experience may qualify for immigration as business immigrants. There are three categories of business immigrants: Investors, Entrepreneurs and Self-Employed Persons.[1] The eligibility requirements under each of these categories are discussed in more detail below.

6:1 THE INVESTOR CATEGORY

In order to qualify for immigration under this particular category, you must:

◆ be an 'Investor' (as defined below);

◆ make a prescribed investment; and

◆ obtain at least the pass mark under the points assessment.

The issues of qualifying as an 'Investor' and that of the prescribed investment are covered immediately below. The topic of the points assessment is discussed in more detail in section 6:4.

[1]Please note as well that some provinces also have their own business immigration programmes. See Chapter 12 for information on Quebec's programme, and Chapter 5 for information relating to the provincial nominee programs generally.

6:1.1 Definition of Investor

An Investor is a person who satisfies the following conditions:

a. has business experience (see below for details regarding this requirement);
b. has a legally obtained net worth[2] of at least CDN $800,000; and
c. indicates in writing to an officer that they intend to make or have made an investment.

Business experience in respect of an Investor means:

i. the management of a qualifying business[3] and the control

---

[2]**Net worth** in respect of an investor means the fair market value of all of the assets of the investor and their spouse or common-law partner minus the fair market value of all of their liabilities.

[3]**Qualifying business** means a business – other than a business operated primarily for the purpose of deriving investment income such as interest, dividends or capital gains – for which, in each of any two years in the period beginning five years before the date of application for a permanent resident visa and ending on the date a determination is made in respect of the application, there is documentary evidence of any two of the following:

a. that the percentage of equity multiplied by the number of full time job equivalents is equal to or greater than two full-time job equivalents per year;

b. that the percentage of equity multiplied by the total annual sales is equal to or greater than CDN$500,000;

c. that the percentage of equity multiplied by the net income (**net income** in respect of a qualifying business or a qualifying Canadian business means the after tax profit or loss of the business plus remuneration by the business to a foreign national and their spouse or common-law partner) in the year is equal to or greater than CDN$50,000; and

d. that the percentage of equity multiplied by the net assets (**net assets** in respect of a qualifying business or a qualifying Canadian business, means the assets of the business, minus the liabilities of the business, plus share-holder loans made to the business by a foreign national and their spouse or common-law partner) at the end of the year is equal to or greater than CDN$125,000.

of a percentage of equity[4] of the qualifying business for at least two years in the period beginning five years before the date of application for a permanent resident visa and ending on the day a determination is made in respect of the application, or

ii. the management of at least five full-time job equivalents[5] per year in a business for at least two years in the period beginning five years before the date of application for a permanent resident visa and ending on the day a determination is made in respect of the application.

6:1.2 The prescribed investment

If you meet the definition of Investor, you must make a prescribed investment, which does not mean that you have to start a business in Canada. What it means is that you will have to invest the sum of CDN$400,000 with the Receiver General of Canada. Approximately five years after you become permanent resident, Citizenship and Immigration Canada (CIC) will return the investment to you, without interest. The investment is fully guaranteed.

It is possible to obtain financing for the prescribed investment. Listed below are details of contact information

---

[4]**Percentage of equity** means
a. in respect of a sole proprietorship, 100% of the equity of the sole proprietorship controlled by a foreign national or their spouse or common-law partner;
b. in respect of a corporation, the percentage of the issued and outstanding voting shares of the capital stock of the corporation controlled by a foreign national or their spouse or common-law partner; and
c. in respect of a partnership or joint venture, the percentage of the profit or loss of the partnership or joint venture to which the foreign national or their spouse or common-law partner is entitled.
[5]**Full-time job equivalent** means, 1,950 hours of paid employment.

relating to a sampling of financial institutions[6] with whom you can make financing arrangements.

Canadian Imperial Bank of Commerce (CIBC)
Mr King H. Lee, Vice-President, Asian Banking
199 Bay Street, Commerce Court West, 5th Floor
Toronto, Ontario, Canada, M5L 1A2
Tel: (416) 980-3513, Fax: (416) 304-5043
E-mail: **King.Lee@cibc.com**
www.cibc.com or **www.cibcasianbanking.com**

Computershare Trust Company of Canada
Mr Charles Eric Gauthier, Corporate Trust Officer
1500 University Street, 7th Floor
Montréal, Quebec, Canada, H3A 3S8
Tel: (514) 982-74888, x7609, Fax: (514) 982-7677
E-mail: **Charles.Gauthier@computershare.com**
www.computershare.com

Desjardins Trust Inc.
Mr Marc Audet, Vice-President
East Tower, 27th Floor, 2 Complexe Desjardins
P.O. Box 992, Station Desjardins, Montréal, Quebec,
  Canada, H5B 1C1
Tel: (514) 499-8440, Fax: (514) 982-9579
E-mail: **cic_inquiry@immigrantinvestor.com**
www.immigrantinvestor.com

[6]This is only a sampling of financial institutions that can assist you with financing. For more contacts, see the site of Canada Deposit Insurance Corporation at **www.cdic.ca**.

Habib Canadian Bank
Mr Laiq Siddiqui, Chief Operating Officer
918 Dundas Street East, Suite 1B
Mississauga, Ontario, Canada, L4Y 4H9
Tel: (905) 276-5300, Fax: (905) 276-5400
E-mail: **laiqhcb@on.aibn.com**
www.habibcanadian.com

HSBC Bank Canada
Mr Eric G. Major, Director, Immigrant Investor
   Programs
P.O. Box 1016, Suite 1100, 885 West Georgia Street
Vancouver, British Columbia, Canada, V6C 3E9
Tel: (604) 631-8086, Fax: (604) 631-8073
E-mail: **Eric_Major@hsbc.ca**
www.hsbc.ca/capital

Laurentian Bank of Canada
Ms Johanne Sheehy, Private Banking
1981 McGill College Ave, Mezzanine Level
Montréal, Quebec, H3A 3K3
Tel: (514) 284-4000, Fax: (514) 284-4009
E-mail: **Johanne.Sheehy@banquelaurentienne.ca**
www.laurentianbank.com/en/02_consumers/
   08_gestion_privee/04_Immigrant/_fr.htm

MCAP Securities Inc.
Mr Paul Bruce
MCAP Securities Inc., Suite 400, 200 King Street West
Toronto, Ontario, Canada, M5H 3T4

Tel: (416) 591-2733, Fax: (416) 598-4142
Toll Free: 1 800 387-4405 ext. 2733
E-mail: **Paul.Bruce@mcap.com**
www.newcanadianplan.com

National Bank of Canada
Mr Fouad Boustani, Manager, Immigrant Investor
  Program
600 De la Gauchetière West, 21st Floor
Montréal, Quebec, Canada, H3B 4L3
Tel: (514) 394-6490, Fax: (514) 394-6915
E-mail: **Fouad.Boustani@bnc.ca**
www.nbc.ca

Scotiabank
Mr Guy Pilote, Associate Director, ScotiaMcLeod,
  Scotia Tower
1002 Sherbrooke Street West, Suite 2140
Montreal, Quebec, Canada H3A 3L6
Tel: (514) 350-776, Fax: (514) 350-7794
E-mail: **guy_pilote@scotiamcleod.com**
www.scotiabank.com/immigrantinvestor

Toronto-Dominion Bank
Mr Ramon Yu, Managing Director
Two Pacific Place, 88 Queensway, Suites 3413–3422
Hong Kong
Tel: (852) 2846-4160, Fax: (852) 2845-9191
E-mail: **Ramon.Yu@td.com**
www.td.com

6:2 THE ENTREPRENEUR CATEGORY

In order to qualify for immigration under this category, you must:

◆ be an 'Entrepreneur' (as defined below);

◆ meet a number of conditions; and

◆ obtain at least the pass mark under the points assessment.

The issues of qualifying as an Entrepreneur and that of the conditions to be met are covered immediately below. The topic of the points assessment is discussed in more detail in section 6:4.

6:2.1 Definition of Entrepreneur

An Entrepreneur is a person who satisfies the following conditions:

a. has business experience, which in respect of an Entrepreneur means the management of a qualifying business[7] and the control of a percentage of equity[8] of the qualifying business for at least two years in the period beginning five years before the date of application for a permanent resident visa and ending on the day a determination is made in respect of the application;

b. has a legally obtained minimum net worth[9] of CDN

---

[7]See footnote 3 above.
[8]See footnote 4 above.
[9]**Net worth** in respect of an Entrepreneur means the fair market value of all of the assets of the Entrepreneur and their spouse or common-law partner minus the fair market value of all of their liabilities.

$300,000 (in respect of an Entrepreneur selected by a province, the minimum net worth required by the laws of the province); and

c. provides a written statement to an officer that they intend to and will be able to meet the conditions[10] referred to in subsections (1) to (4), which can be found immediately below.

(1) An Entrepreneur who becomes a permanent resident must meet the following conditions:

a. the Entrepreneur must control a percentage of the equity of a qualifying Canadian business[11] equal to or greater than $33^1/3\%$;

b. the Entrepreneur must provide active and ongoing management of the qualifying Canadian business; and

---

[10]Please note that all family members are admitted under the same conditions as the principal applicant; the conditions are removed once the Entrepreneur satisfies them.

[11]**Qualifying Canadian business** means a business operated in Canada by an entrepreneur – other than a business primarily for the purpose of deriving investment income, such as interest, dividends or capital gains – for which there is in any year within the period of three years after the day the entrepreneur becomes a permanent resident documentary evidence of any two of the following:

a. the percentage of equity multiplied by the number of full time job equivalents is equal to or greater than two full-time job equivalents per year;

b. the percentage of equity multiplied by the total annual sales is equal to or greater than CDN$250,000;

c. the percentage of equity multiplied by the net income (which, in respect of a qualifying business or a qualifying Canadian business, means the after tax profit or loss of the business plus remuneration by the business to a foreign national and their spouse or common-law partner) in the year is equal to or greater than CDN$25,000; and

d. the percentage of equity multiplied by the net assets (which, in respect of a qualifying business or a qualifying Canadian business, means the assets of the business, minus the liabilities of the business, plus shareholder loans made to the business by a foreign national and their spouse or common-law partner) at the end of the year is equal to or greater than CDN$125,000.

c. the Entrepreneur must create at least one incremental full-time job equivalent for Canadian citizens or permanent residents, other than the entrepreneur and their family members.

(2) The Entrepreneur must meet the conditions for a period of at least one year within the period of three years after the day on which the Entrepreneur becomes a permanent resident.

(3) An Entrepreneur who becomes a permanent resident must provide to an officer evidence of compliance with the conditions within the period of three years after the day on which the Entrepreneur becomes a permanent resident.

(4) An Entrepreneur must provide to an officer:

a. not later than six months after the day on which the Entrepreneur becomes a permanent resident, their residential address and telephone number; and
b. during the period beginning 18 months after and ending 24 months after the day on which the Entrepreneur becomes a permanent resident, evidence of their efforts to comply with the conditions.

6:3 THE SELF-EMPLOYED CATEGORY

In order to qualify for immigration under this category, a person must:

◆ be 'Self-Employed' (as defined below); and

◆ obtain at least the pass mark under the points assessment.

The topic of the points assessment is discussed in more detail in section 6:4.

A Self-Employed person is one who:

a. has relevant experience[11], and
b. has the intention and ability to create their own employ-ment and make a significant contribution in Canada in the fields of cultural activities or athletics, or purchase and manage a farm in Canada.

You must also have the intention and ability to establish a business that will, at a minimum, create employment for yourself. No immigration conditions are imposed on this class. You must have enough money to support yourself and your family members after you arrive in Canada.

6:4 THE POINTS ASSESSMENT

In Chapter 3 of this book you were introduced to the points system used by CIC in assessing immigration applications. As mentioned above, to qualify under all of the busi-ness immigration categories (Investor, Entrepreneur and

[12]**Relevant experience** in respect of a Self-Employed person means at least two years in the period beginning five years before the date of application for a permanent resident visa and ending on the day a determination is made in respect of the application, in the following types of experience:
i. self-employment in cultural activities or in athletics, and
ii. participation at a world-class level in cultural activities or athletics, or
iii. farm management experience.

Self-Employed), you must meet the requisite definitions and also obtain at least the pass mark under the points assessment. Some of the issues set out in Chapter 3 are the same as those for business applications, but a full discussion of issues is provided in the context of this chapter. See also, however, Chapter 3 for analysis of any duplicated issues.

The pass mark is variable and is determined, on an ongoing basis, by CIC. Currently, the pass mark in business cases is 35 points. At the time of making your application you should, however, check to see if this number has changed.

The points assessment is made against five selection factors: business experience, age, education, English and French language ability and adaptability. Shown below is a self-assessment table, followed by charts relevant to the business experience, education and language skills, which are common to all three categories. Figure 13 contains the tables pertaining to the factors of Age and Adaptability for Investors and Entrepreneurs, and Figure 14 has the tables relevant to Age and Adaptability for Self-Employed persons.

Factor		Maximum points	Your score
1	Business experience/ Relevant experience	35	
2	Age	10	
3	Education	25	
4	Language proficiency	24	
5	Adaptability	6	
	Total	**100**	

Factor 1: Business experience (maximum 35 points)

Business experience must have been obtained within the period beginning five years before the date of application.

Two years business experience	20
Three years business experience	25
Four years business experience	30
Five years business experience	35

Factor 3: Education (maximum 25 points)

You have not completed secondary school (also called high school)	0
You have obtained a secondary school credential	5
You have obtained a one-year post-secondary educational credential and completed at least 12 years of full-time or full-time equivalent studies	12
You have obtained a one-year post-secondary educational credential and completed at least 13 years of full-time or full-time equivalent studies	15
You have obtained a one-year university credential at the Bachelor's level and completed at least 13 years of full-time or full-time equivalent studies	15
You have obtained a two-year post-secondary educational credential and completed at least 14 years of full-time or full-time equivalent studies	20
You have obtained a two-year educational credential at the Bachelor's level and completed at least 14 years of full-time or full-time equivalent studies	20
You have obtained a three-year post-secondary educational credential and completed at least 15 years of full-time or full-time equivalent studies	22
You have obtained two or more university educational credentials at the Bachelor's level and completed at least 15 years of full-time or full-time equivalent studies	22
You have obtained a Master's or PhD and completed at least 17 years of full-time or full-time equivalent studies	25

Fig. 13.   Chart for Investors and Entrepreneurs.

Factor 4: English and French language ability (maximum 24 points)

To assess your English and French language ability, first decide which language you are most comfortable with. This language is your first official language. The language you feel less comfortable communicating with is your second official language. Next, award points according to your ability to read, write, listen to and speak English and French. The following two tables define the levels of language proficiency and how points are allotted for each level.

Skill level	Criteria
High proficienty	You can communicate effectively in most community and workplace situations. You speak, listen to, read and write the language very well.
Moderate proficiency	You can make yourself understood and you understand what others are saying in most workplace and community situations. You speak, listen to, read and write the language well.
Basic proficiency	You do not meet the above criteria for moderate proficiency but still have some ability to speak, listen to, read or write the language.
No proficiency	You have no ability whatsoever in speaking, listening to, reading or writing the language.

Fig. 13. continued.

Calculating your language points

First official language	Read	Write	Listen	Speak	Maximum score per category
High proficiency	4	4	4	4	16
Moderate proficiency	2	2	2	2	8
Basic proficiency	1	1	1	1	2
No proficiency	0	0	0	0	0
Maximum possible score for all four abilities in first official language =					16

Second official language	Read	Write	Listen	Speak	Maximum score per category
High proficiency	2	2	2	2	8
Moderate proficiency	2	2	2	2	8
Basic proficiency	1	1	1	1	2
No proficiency	0	0	0	0	0
Maximum possible score for all four abilities in second official language =					8
Maximum possible score total for both official languages =					24

Factor 2: Age (maximum 10 points)
Investors/Entrepreneurs only

Points are given for your age at the time your application is received.

Age	Total points
16 or under	0
17	2
18	4
19	6
20	8
21–49	10
50	8
51	6
52	4
53	2
54 and over	0

Fig. 13. continued.

Factor 5: Adaptability (maximum 6 points)
Investors/Entrepreneurs only

A maximum of 6 points for adaptability can be earned by any combination of the following elements:

You have made a business exploration trip to Canada in the period beginning five years before the date of your application	6
You have participated in joint federal-provincial business immigration initiatives	6

If you wish to be assessed for adaptability points, it is necessary that your province of destination provides you with documentation indicating that it is satisfied that you have met one or both of the above elements.

For the purpose of awarding points:

a. a trip to Canada becomes a business exploration trip to Canada only when a province has deemed it to be so; and

b. each province establishes individually what constitutes participation in a joint federal-provincial business immigration initiative.

Fig. 13. continued.

Factor 2: Age (maximum 10 points) Self-employed only

Points are given for your age at the time your application is received.

Age	Total points
16 or under	0
17	2
18	4
19	6

Fig. 14. Chart for Self-Employed persons.

20	8
21–49	10
50	8
51	6
52	4
53	2
54 and over	0

Factor 5: Adaptability (maximum 6 points)
Self-employed only

A maximum of 6 points for adaptability can be earned by any combination of the following elements:

1. Your accompanying spouse or common-law partner's level of education

Secondary school (high school) diploma or less	0
A one or two-year post-secondary educational credential and at least 13 years of education	3
A three-year post-secondary educational credential and at least 15 years of education	4
A three-year university credential and at least 15 years of education	4
A Master's or PhD and at least 17 years of education	5

2. You or your accompanying spouse or common-law partner has studied in Canada

Not at all, or anything less than two years post-secondary education in Canada	0
Obtained a Canadian post-secondary educational credential of at least two years since the age of 18	5

3. You or your accompanying spouse or common-law partner has worked in Canada

Not at all, or less than one year full-time work in Canada	0
Worked full-time in Canada for at least one year	5

Fig. 14. continued.

4. You or your accompanying spouse or common-law partner has family in Canada

No   0

Have a parent, grandparent, aunt, uncle, sister, brother, nephew, niece, child or grandchild who is a Canadian citizen or permanent resident living in Canada   5

Fig. 14. continued.

6:5 APPLYING FOR PERMANENT RESIDENCE UNDER THE BUSINESS IMMIGRANTS CLASS

You can download the forms online as mentioned in Chapter 1. For a sample checklist of the forms and documents that have to be submitted, see Figure 15.

You must chose to apply under only one of the three categories, even if you meet the requirements for more than one category. Note that you cannot change the class you are applying under once you have submitted your application.

The second step is to submit the completed application and fees to the relevant visa office.[13] Once your application is successful, you and your family members may be required to attend an interview.

If you have applied as an Investor, once all immigration matters have been addressed you must sign a subscription agreement[14] and pay the required investment. You must pay your investment within 30 days after receiving notification

[13]See Schedule 1 (page 219).
[14]You can review the content of a subscription agreement at **www.cic.gc.ca/english/pdf/pub/busagr-irpa.pdf**.

Checklist

Assemble all your documents as listed. Check (☑) each applicable item on the checklist and attach the checklist to your documents (a paper clip will do). Place all the documents in a sealed envelope.

Do not send originals. Send photocopies of all documents, **except** the *Certificat de sélection du Québec (CSQ)*, if your intention is to live in the province of Quebec, and the police certificates, which must be **originals**. If your documents are not in English or French, send a notarized (certified) translation with a copy of the originals.

If you are unable to provide any of the requested documentation for special reasons, please attach a **written explanation** with full details as to why that documentation is unavailable.

1.	**APPLICATION FORMS**
	Check that it is completed, signed and dated. Your signed application should include:
	• *Application for Permanent Residence in Canada* with a stapled envelope containing photos. ☐
	• *Schedule 1 - Background / Declaration* completed and signed by you and each of your family members 18 years or older. ☐
	• *Schedule 6 - Economic Classes - Business Immigrants* completed. ☐
	• *Additional Family Information* completed by you, your spouse or common-law partner and each dependent child aged 18 or over (whether accompanying you or not). ☐
	If you want us to deal with a Canadian representative on your behalf, be sure you have completed and signed the *Authority to Release Information to Designated Individuals* form. ☐
2.	**IDENTITY AND CIVIL STATUS DOCUMENTS** ☐
	Birth, marriage, final divorce, annulment or separation certificates for you and spouse; death certificate for former spouse if applicable.
3.	**CHILDREN'S INFORMATION** ☐
	Children's birth certificates (which name their parents); adoption papers for adopted dependent children; proof of custody for children under the age of 22 and proof that the children may be removed from the jurisdiction of the court; if the children will not accompany you to Canada, proof that you have fulfilled any obligation stated in custody agreements. Statutory declaration that the remaining father or mother has no objection to the child living in Canada.
4.	**POLICE CERTIFICATES AND CLEARANCES** ☐
	Police certificates or clearances from each country in which you and everyone in your family aged 18 years or over have lived six months or more since reaching 18 years of age. **You must attach the original police document(s).** If these certificates are in a language other than English or French, they must be accompanied by a certified translation in either English or French.
5.	**BACKGROUND DOCUMENTS (IF APPLICABLE)** ☐
	Any document to support your answers to questions in the *Background/Declaration* form such as completion of military service card, military records, membership cards or any documents showing your association or involvement in any social, political, vocational and cultural organization.

Fig. 15.   Sample checklist of documents for business immigrants.

6.	**TRAVEL DOCUMENTS AND PASSPORTS**	☐
	Passports or travel documents for yourself, your spouse and dependent children. Include only copies of pages showing the passport number, date of issue and expiration, your photo, name, date and place of birth. If you live in a country other than your country of nationality, include a copy of your visa for the country in which you currently live.	
7.	**SETTLEMENT FUNDS**	☐
	You must provide proof of sufficient funds currently available to maintain yourself and your family members until you are self-supporting in Canada. These funds must be readily transferable to Canada in a convertible currency. Financial statements for the last three (3) years (bank accounts, shares certificates, portfolio, etc.). Proof of assets (properties, buildings, lands, etc.). **Note:** If you carry more than $10,000 Canadian in cash funds upon your entry to Canada, you will have to disclose these funds to a Canadian official upon arrival. Cash funds means money (coins or bank notes), securities in bearer form (stocks, bonds, debentures, treasury bills, etc.) and negotiable instruments in bearer form (bankers drafts, cheques, travellers' cheques, money orders, etc.). Failure to disclose can result in fines and imprisonment.	
8.	**FEE PAYMENT**	☐
	Consult the Web site of the visa office to which you will be applying to find out the acceptable method for paying the fees. **Do not enclose cash**. You must submit the acceptable fee payment **with** your completed application. See the **Fees** section in this guide.	
9.	**CERTIFICAT DE SÉLECTION DU QUÉBEC (CSQ)**	☐
	Original of the *Certificat de sélection du Québec (CSQ)* if your intention is to live in the province of Québec.	
10.	**ADDITIONAL INFORMATION**	☐
	Any document or record to demonstrate your adaptability, initiative, motivation, or resourcefulness. All school certificates, diplomas and degrees for you and your spouse or common-law partner (if applicable), including apprenticeship or trade papers. Letters of reference or work certificates from present and past employers for you and your spouse or common-law partner.	
11.	**PHOTOS**	☐
	Provide the correct number of photographs specified on the Web site of the visa office to which you are applying (follow the links from www.cic.gc.ca) and follow the instructions provided in **Appendix C: Photo Specifications.**	

Fig. 15. continued.

from the relevant visa office. Your immigrant visa will not be issued unless the payment is made.

Your payment should include:

◆ your name (must be the same as the one on your form);

◆ your address;

◆ your immigration file number (B number);

◆ the location of the visa office that is processing your application; and

◆ two signed copies of the subscription agreement.

After you have paid your investment, you or your financial institution will receive a copy of the subscription agreement and the promissory note.

If you decide that you do not want to be an Investor but you have already made your payment, you must immediately contact the visa office processing your case and CIC headquarters in Ottawa to get your full investment back. Your investment will not be refunded if you have been issued a permanent resident visa.

If your application is not approved, you can request a refund of your investment. You will get your investment back within 90 days of requesting a refund.

Lastly, with regard to the business immigration category, please note that many provinces provide valuable information and services to assist business immigrants in setting up and successfully operating businesses in Canada. You can contact provincial and territorial governments (see the list of addresses below) and also CIC at their Business Immigration headquarters in Ottawa:

Director, Business Immigration
Citizenship and Immigration Canada
Jean Edmonds Tower North, 7th Floor
300 Slater Street, Ottawa, Ontario, Canada, K1A 1L1
Fax: 613-941-9014,
E-mail: **Nat-Business-Immigration@cic.gc.ca**

Alberta
Business Immigration Program
Alberta Economic Development
4th Floor, Commerce Place
10155-102 Street
Edmonton, Alberta
Canada T5J 4L6
Tel: (780) 427-6419, Fax: (780) 422-9127
www.alberta-canada.com/bip

British Columbia
British Columbia Business Immigration
Ministry of Competition, Science and Enterprise
730-999 Canada Place
Vancouver, British Columbia
Canada V6C 3E1
Tel: (604) 844-1900, Fax: (604) 660-4092
www.cse.gov.bc.ca/Subwebs/BusImm/

Manitoba
Department of Industry, Trade and Tourism
410-155 Carleton Street
Winnipeg, Manitoba
Canada R3C 3H8
Tel: (204) 945-2466, Fax: (204) 957-1793
www.gov.mb.ca/itt/trade

New Brunswick
Business New Brunswick
P.O. Box 6000
Fredericton, New Brunswick
Canada E3B 5H1
Tel: (506) 453-3981, Fax: (506) 444-4277
www.gnb.ca/immigration/english/
  invest/business.htm

Newfoundland and Labrador
Trade and Investment Division
Industry, Trade and Technology
P.O. Box 8700
St John's, Newfoundland
Canada A1B 4J6
Tel: (709) 729-2781, Fax: (709) 729-5936
www.success.nfld.net

Northwest Territories
Investment Development, Trade and Investment
  Division
Department of Resources, Wildlife and Economic
  Development
Government of the Northwest Territories
P.O. Box 1320, 3rd Floor
Northern United Place
Yellowknife, Northwest Territories
Canada X1A 2L9
Tel: (867) 920-8969, Fax: (867) 873-0101
www.rwed.gov.nt.ca

Nova Scotia
Business Immigration
Nova Scotia Economic Development and Tourism
Business Development Corporation
P.O. Box 519
1800 Argyle Street, Suite 601
Halifax, Nova Scotia
Canada B3J 2R7
Tel: (902) 424-6864, Fax: (902) 424-6823
www.novascotiabusiness.com

Nunavut
Department of Sustainable Development
Government of Nunavut
P.O. Box 1340
Iqaluit, Nunavut
Canada X0A 0H0
Tel: (867) 979-5070, Fax: (867) 979-5920
www.gov.nu.ca

Ontario
Manager, Business Immigration Section
Investment Branch
Ministry of Economic Development and Trade
Hearst Block, 5th Floor, 900 Bay Street
Toronto, Ontario
Canada M7A 2E1
Tel: (416) 325-6986, Fax: (416) 325-6653
www.2ontario.com/bi/home.asp

Prince Edward Island
Immigration Investment and Trade Policy Division
Department of Development and Technology
P.O. Box 1176
94 Euston Street, 2nd Floor
Charlottetown, Prince Edward Island
Canada C1A 7M8
Tel: (902) 894-0351, Fax: (902) 368-5886
www.gov.pe.ca

Quebec
Ministère des Relations avec les citoyens et de
l'Immigration
Direction de l'aide à l'immigration d'affaires
415, rue St-Roch
Montréal (Québec)
Canada H3N 1K2
Tel: (514) 864-9191, Fax: (514) 864-3825
www.immigration-quebec.gouv.qc.ca/anglais/
business/business-quebec.html

Saskatchewan

Saskatchewan Government Relations and Aboriginal
  Affairs

2nd Floor, Office Tower

Delta Regina

1919 Saskatchewan Drive

Regina, Saskatchewan

Canada S4P 3V7

Tel: (306) 787-9212, Fax: (306) 787-3872

www.graa.gov.sk.ca

Yukon

Industry, Trade and Investment

Department of Economic Development

P.O. Box 2703, Suite 400

211 Main Street

Whitehorse, Yukon

Canada Y1A 2C6

Tel: (867) 667-5466, Fax: (867) 667-8601

www.economicdevelopment.gov.yk.ca

7

Application for a Work Permit[1]

If you are interested in working[2] temporarily in Canada, you have to apply for, and meet, the requirements of a work permit. You must also meet the requirements generally related to temporary residence in Canada, which are discussed in more detail in Chapter 9.

You may be particularly interested in acquiring work experience in Canada if you foresee that you may one day apply for permanent residence – Canadian work experience is an important factor in a skilled worker permanent residence application, covered in Chapter 3.

7:1 THE STEPS INVOLVED IN OBTAINING A WORK PERMIT
The following are the key issues in obtaining a work permit:

a. An employer must offer you a job.

---

[1]**A work permit** is a written authorisation to work in Canada issued by an officer to a person who is not a Canadian citizen or a permanent resident of Canada. It is required whether or not the employer is in Canada. Usually it is valid only for a specified job and length of time.
[2]**Work** is an activity for which wages or commission is earned, or that competes directly with activities of Canadian citizens or permanent residents in the Canadian Labour Market.

b. Human Resources and Skills Development Canada (HRSDC) will provide an opinion as to whether a foreign national may take the job, unless you qualify for HRSDC exemption[3], in which case you will not have to obtain and submit an HRSDC opinion.

c. You may then apply for a work permit.

Before discussing in more detail the three steps mentioned above, it should be noted that there are certain categories of employment for which **one does not need a work permit issued by Citizenship and Immigration Canada (CIC)**. These particular categories are listed below in Figure 16.

Business visitors

People coming to Canada on business do not need a work permit. Business visitors must work for a company located outside of Canada. Business visitors cannot directly enter the Canadian labour market.

Foreign representatives

Diplomats and official representatives of other countries or the United Nations, and their staff, do not need a work permit to work in Canada.

Family members of foreign representatives

Family members of accredited diplomats may work in Canada without a permit if they have a 'no objection letter' from the Canadian Department of Foreign Affairs and International Trade.

Fig. 16. Work permit exempt categories.

[3]See section 7:1.2(b) for more details.

Military personnel

Members of an armed force from another country may work in Canada without a permit if they possess movement orders that state that they are entering Canada under the terms of the Visiting Forces Act.

Foreign government officers

Canada has exchange agreements with some countries for public officials to work in each other's government departments. Government officials coming to work in Canada should bring a formal letter of agreement if their period of work is longer than three months.

On-campus employment

Certain foreign students studying in Canada can work on their campus without a work permit.

Performing artists

Foreign artists and their essential supporting staff coming to Canada to perform do not need a permit if they are only performing in Canada for a limited period of time and will not be performing in a bar or restaurant. Artists working in Canada in this category may not enter into an employment relationship with the Canadian group that has contracted for their services. Artists must also not perform for the production of a movie, television or radio broadcast.

Athletes and coaches

Foreign teams, athletes and coaches may compete in Canada without a work permit.

Fig. 16. continued.

News reporters

Reporters working for foreign newspapers, television channels, news agencies, or companies involved in reporting news events may work in Canada to report on events in Canada.

Public speakers

Guest speakers, commercial speakers or seminar leaders may speak or deliver training in Canada without a work permit as long as the event is not longer than five days.

Convention organisers

Organisers and administrative staff who are organising meetings or conventions in Canada do not need a work permit.

Note: service providers, such as those who provide audio-visual services and other such 'hands-on' help, do need a work permit to work in Canada.

Clergy

Persons who are coming to Canada to work as ordained ministers, lay persons or members of a religious order, do not need a work permit to perform their religious duties or assist a religious group. These religious duties may include preaching doctrine, presiding at liturgical functions or spiritual counselling.

Fig. 16. continued.

Judges and referees

Officials at international amateur competitions may come to Canada to judge or officiate without a work permit.

Examiners and evaluators

Professors and academic experts may come to Canada to evaluate or supervise academic projects, research proposals or university theses. This applies to Canadian research organisations as well as academic institutions.

Expert witnesses or investigators

Experts may work in Canada without a work permit to give evidence for a regulatory body, tribunal or court of law.

Health care students

Foreign health-care students can do their clinical clerkships or short-term work in Canada without a work permit if the work is for the primary purpose of acquiring training. Health care students must have written approval from the Canadian regulatory board responsible for their occupation. A normal training *practicum* should not exceed four months.

Note: Although a work permit is not required, a Canadian Immigration medical exam is required before entry.

Fig. 16. continued.

Civil aviation inspector

Inspectors coming to Canada to do safety inspections of flight operations or cabin safety of commercial airlines doing international flights do not need a work permit.

Accident or incident inspector

Accredited representatives or advisors coming to Canada do not need a work permit to work as part of an aviation accident or incident investigation conducted under the authority of the Transportation Accident Investigation and Safety Board Act.

Crew members

Foreign members of a crew working on foreign vehicles (for example: flight attendants or shipping crew) do not need a work permit if the vehicle is in Canada for the international transportation of cargo or passengers.

Emergency service providers

Persons coming into Canada to help out in emergencies do not need a work permit if they are entering to help preserve life or property. Examples of emergencies would be natural disasters such as floods or earthquakes, or industrial accidents threatening the environment.

Fig. 16. continued.

7:1.1 The job offer

To get to the point of receiving an offer from a Canadian employer, you must obviously first go through the steps that were discussed in Chapter 2: research the jobs available and potential employers, prepare your cover letters and resumés, and apply for jobs. If a Canadian employer wishes to hire you, then the employer must make you a formal job offer. The job offer can be a written letter or a more formal employment contract.

7:1.2 The HRSDC process

Once an offer is secured, your employer must, unless you qualify for HRSDC exemption (see section 7:1.2(b)), seek 'confirmation' from HRSDC. The employer must provide to HRSDC the following information in order to seek confirmation:

◆ the title of the job offered;

◆ a description of the duties and responsibilities of the position offered;

◆ a list of education, skills and experience that a worker must have in order to fulfil the job requirements; a list of the licences and professional credentials required should also be included;

◆ the start and end dates for the position to be filled; please note that the position must be offered for a limited time, it cannot be held by the foreign national indefinitely;

◆ information regarding the salary that is being offered, including wages and other forms of payment (for example: room and board or commission);[4]

---

[4]Note that it is imperative that the wages and working conditions be appropriate for the industry.

◆ the name and address of the employer, and the address where the foreign worker will be working; the offer should also include the name and phone number of a contact at the business who is who is familiar with the job offer, so that CIC and HRSDC can make the necessary inquiries.

As noted above, in order for you to qualify for a work permit, the offer of employment must be one of temporary employment, meaning for a definite period of time. Note that if you intend to apply, or have already applied for permanent residence in Canada, an employer may make you an offer of indeterminate employment. Please see Chapter 3 in this regard.

If you need to get a better sense of the information that needs to be provided to HRSDC, see Figure 17 for a sample temporary foreign worker application form.

7:1.2.a HRSDC's considerations

HRSDC is involved in this process for two reasons. First, they will assess the genuineness of the offer of employment. Secondly, HRSDC will weigh the likely effect that the employment of a foreign national will have on the Canadian labour market. If HRSDC is satisfied on these issues, they will then issue an opinion (also known as 'confirmation') advising CIC with regard to this matter.

Under current law, which came into effect in June 2002, the considerations of HRSDC have broadened as compared to previous law; they now include the following:

**Human Resources
Development Canada**   Développement des
ressources humaines Canada

Please Print
PROTECTED WHEN COMPLETED - B

TEMPORARY FOREIGN WORKER APPLICATION

TYPE OF REQUEST

☐ Temporary Employment   ☐ Renewal / Extension

EMPLOYER INFORMATION

Business name		Telephone Number ( ) –

Name of business owner

Business Address: Number and Street	City	Province	Postal Code

Is this a head office? ☐ Yes ☐ No	Canada Customs and Revenue Agency (CCRA) business number	Date business started (yyyy-mm-dd)	Website

Describe the principal business activity:

Location of employment of prospective employee(s) if different from employer's address

Number and Street	City	Province	Postal Code

Number of employees in Canada	Number of Canadians / permanent residents employed	Number of foreign workers currently employed (neither Canadian citizens nor permanent residents)	Were any employees laid off in the past 12 months? ☐ No ☐ Yes If yes, how many?

Reason(s) for layoff(s) and occupations affected:

CONTACT INFORMATION

Name of Business Contact	Address Number and Street if different from above:	City	Province	Postal Code

Job Title	Telephone Number ( ) –	Fax Number ( ) –	E-mail

* THIRD PARTY INFORMATION (if applicable)

Third Party Agent authorized to act for employer	Company Name of Agent

Address: Number and Street	City	Province	Postal Code

Telephone Number ( ) –	Fax Number ( ) –	E-mail	Website

* If you are a third party agent acting on behalf of an employer, written authorization from the employer to act on his/her behalf is required and should
  * normally be presented on the employer's original company letterhead;
  * be signed by an official with signing authority for the employer;
  * specifically authorize the agent to act on the employer's behalf in obtaining a labour market opinion from Human Resources Development Canada (HRDC); and
  * state any limitations of authority to act on the employer's behalf (duration, specific situations etc.)

HRDC reserves the right to contact the employer directly if necessary.

EMP5239 (04-02) E   Aussi disponible en français

Canadä

Fig. 17.   Sample temporary foreign worker application form.

INFORMATION ON JOB OFFER

Provide detailed information for the position. Use a separate sheet for positions with different requirements.

Occupation	Job title within your organization

Requirements of the job. Provide details.

a) provincial / territorial accreditation, certification, licensing or registration requirements:

b) educational / knowledge requirements:

c) experience:

d) skills:

e) language requirements:

☐ English   ☐ French   ☐ Other   If "Other", please explain.

Duties the worker will perform and any working conditions specific to the job:

Is this occupation regulated by a professional association or licensing body?

☐ No   ☐ Yes ➔ If yes, what is the name of the association?

Has the association been consulted about the hiring of a foreign worker ?   ☐ No   ☐ Yes

Has the association raised any objections to the hiring of a foreign worker ?

☐ No   ☐ Yes ➔ If yes, provide details.

Is the position part of a union (bargaining unit) ?

☐ No   ☐ Yes ➔ If yes, what is the name of the union?

Has the union been consulted about the hiring of a foreign worker?   ☐ No   ☐ Yes

What is the position of the union? Provide details. Attach documentation, if available.

Would hiring a foreign worker affect the settlement of any labour dispute in progress at the place of employment?

☐ No   ☐ Yes ➔ If yes, provide details

Anticipated duration of employment (yyyy-mm-dd)

Start date   End date

Salary (in Canadian dollars) (not including gratuities, commission, room and board).				Number of hours per day	Number of days per week
$___ per hour $___ per day $___ per month $___ per yea					

Other benefits (in Canadian dollars):

gratuities $___   bonuses $___   commissions $___   room & board $___   paid holidays ___

☐ disability insurance   ☐ medical insurance   ☐ dental insurance   ☐ pension   Other: ___

EMP5239 (04-02) E   2

Fig. 17. continued.

RATIONALE FOR REQUEST

Why do you need to hire a foreign worker?

How did you fill this position in the past?

Have you attempted to recruit Canadians / permanent residents?　☐ No　☐ Yes

If yes, provide details of your recruitment efforts and the results.
Attach supporting documentation such as advertising copy, letters, industry consultations, etc.
If no, please explain.

Approximately how many foreign workers have you recruited in the last 5 years?

How does the foreign worker fit into your business / human resource plan?

What are the potential benefits to the labour market in Canada that will occur as a result of employing the foreign worker?
☐ filling a labour shortage　☐ retention of employees who might otherwise be laid off　☐ transfer of new skills and knowledge to Canadians / permanent residents　☐ direct job creation　☐ other

Provide details:

Do you plan to train Canadians / permanent residents for the position to be filled by the foreign worker?　☐ No　☐ Yes

If yes, provide a brief description of the training plan.　If no, please explain.

EMP5239 (04-02) E

3

Fig. 17. continued.

FOREIGN WORKER INFORMATION

How many workers are you requesting with this application? **Provide information for each worker coming into Canada on a separate sheet.**

Family name		Given Name(s)	

☐ Male ☐ Female | Date of birth (yyyy-mm-dd) | Country of birth | Citizenship

Current address Number and Street of foreign worker: | City | | Province | Country | Postal Code

If the foreign worker is currently in Canada, please indicate the immigration status:

☐ temporary resident without a work permit   ☐ foreign worker with a work permit   ☐ refugee claimant   ☐ student   ☐ spouse of a Canadian   ☐ other (please specify) _____

Immigration document expiry date (yyyy-mm-dd) | At which immigration post will the foreign worker(s) likely be processed?

Does the foreign worker have the required job qualifications to work in Canada?

☐ Yes ☐ No → If no, explain how you plan to address the gap.

Does the foreign worker have any financial interests in, or other attachments to, the business?

☐ No ☐ Yes

Is the foreign worker related to anyone in this organization?   ☐ No ☐ Yes

RENEWAL/EXTENSION INFORMATION

Please provide the original HRDC system file number.

Attach a copy of the foreign worker's current work permit (Employment Authorization).

Please provide the reason(s) for the request for an extension.

Have there been significant changes to the business since the original request for a temporary foreign worker?

☐ No ☐ Yes → If yes, have these changes affected the foreign worker?

Have the conditions of the original approval of the job offer been met?

☐ Yes - demonstrate how this is the case   ☐ No - provide details

If one of the conditions was a training plan, provide a detailed progress report.

What recruitment efforts have been undertaken for the position since the foreign worker was first hired? Submit documentation and explain the results of your efforts.

What is your long-term plan for this foreign worker?

Fig. 17. continued.

DECLARATION OF EMPLOYER

I understand that personal information about the temporary foreign worker(s) will be shared by HRDC with Citizenship and Immigration Canada (CIC) and may be shared with other federal/provincial/territorial departments and their agencies to support the application of the foreign worker(s) for a work permit.

I understand that all other information found in the application (except personal information about the temporary foreign worker(s)) will also be shared by HRDC with CIC and may be shared with federal/provincial/territorial departments and their agencies as well as municipal governments, unions and associations and other appropriate organizations to ensure employers are meeting the requirements to hire temporary foreign workers under immigration legislation.

This information may be used for research, evaluation and/or policy analysis.

I/We certify that the information contained in this application is true and accurate.

_____   _____
Signature of Authorized Official or Third Party Representative   Title of Authorized Official

_____   _____
Name of Employer   Date (yyyy-mm-dd)

INFORMATION FOR EMPLOYERS

Completion of this form is voluntary; however, failure to provide any of the requested information may mean your request for a foreign worker will be turned down. Normally your application will be processed within 15 working days from the time all required information has been provided to HRDC.

You may submit a request to HRDC to view the information provided on the application form pursuant to the *Privacy Act*. Instructions for making formal requests are provided in the publication, *Info Source*, copies of which are available at Human Resource Centres of Canada or on the web at: http://infosource.gc.ca/
When requesting information, refer to Personal Information Bank number HRDC PPU 440.

Please forward this application to the nearest
Human Resources Centre of Canada (HRCC) responsible for processing foreign worker applications.
For the list of appropriate HRCCs consult the National Foreign Worker website at:

http://www.hrdc-drhc.gc.ca/hrib/lmd-dmt/fw-te/

or

Consult the blue pages of your telephone directory under Government of Canada. Once an Officer approves this application, the employer will be notified. The foreign worker must then apply to Citizenship and Immigration Canada.

Fig. 17. continued.

◆ whether the work is likely to result in direct job creation or job retention for Canadian citizens or permanent residents;

◆ whether the work is likely to result in the creation or transfer of skills and knowledge for the benefit of Canadian citizens of permanent residents;

◆ whether the work is likely to fill a labour shortage;

◆ whether the wages and working conditions offered are sufficient to attract Canadian citizens or permanent residents to, and retain them in, that work;

◆ whether the employer has made, or has agreed to make, reasonable efforts to hire or train Canadian citizens or permanent residents;

◆ whether the employment of the foreign national is likely to adversely affect the settlement of any labour dispute in progress or the employment of any person involved in the dispute.

If HRSDC issues a 'confirmation'/market opinion letter,[5] you can then apply for a work permit. The employer should advise you if and when HRSDC confirms that you, a foreign national, may fill the job. The employer should also provide you with a copy of the opinion letter from HRSDC. You will include it, together with a copy of the formal job offer, in your application to CIC for a work permit.

---

[5]The HRSDC confirmation is typically given for a specific period of time, and the work permit will be issued to coincide with this period.

7:1.2b HRSDC confirmation-exempt work permit applicants
There are certain categories of **temporary workers who do not need to obtain and submit HRSDC opinions** in order to apply for work permits. Please find below a description of some of the more common HRSDC-exempt work permit applications.

7:1.2b(i) International agreements
There are various agreements allowing entry of certain persons to work in Canada. Certainly, the most frequently used is the North American Free Trade Agreement (NAFTA), which provides for American and Mexican professionals, traders, investors and others to work in Canada without a confirmation from HRSDC. Other such agreements include GATS (General Agreement on Trade in Services) and CCFTA (Canada – Chile Free Trade Agreement) which provide similar benefits for other nationalities. Please see Schedule 10 (page 250) for a list of GATS signatory members.

7:1.2b(ii) Intra-company transfers
Intra-company transferees are persons being transferred by corporations with branches in Canada and abroad. Such persons must have one year of experience in the company as an executive, manager, or as a person with specialised knowledge in the field. Intra-company transferee provisions may fall under GATS, NAFTA, CCFTA or the general regulatory provisions (IRPR).

7:1.2b(iii) Significant benefit
Under this broad category there are various situations where CIC may forego confirmation from HRSDC. For instance,

certain religious workers, entrepreneurs, researchers and people whose employment may provide reciprocal benefit to Canadians may qualify under this category.

7:2 APPLYING FOR A WORK PERMIT

In most cases, you must apply for a work permit at a visa office abroad. In some cases you may apply at a port of entry, or inside Canada. The following are the considerations in determining where you may apply.

7:2.1 Applying for a work permit at a port of entry

You can apply at the port of entry/border if:

a. you are a citizen of the USA, Greenland or St Pierre and Miquelon; or

b. you are a person who does not need a temporary resident visa to come to Canada (see Schedule 3 on p. 227) and the job you will be doing in Canada does not require confirmation from HRSDC (see section 7:1.2b above).

7:2.2 Applying for a work permit from inside Canada

You may also make an inland[6] application for a work permit if:

a. you or your parents have a study permit or work permit; or

b. you are authorised to do one particular job in Canada without a work permit, and you want to obtain a permit to do another job; in that case, you can apply for the work permit within Canada provided that:

[6]It means from within Canada.

i. you have worked in Canada for three months in a row, and

ii. you are not a business visitor (for more information on business visitors, see Figure 16); or

c. you have a temporary resident permit that is valid for six or more months, or

d. you are in Canada because you have an inland application for permanent residence (please note that in this case you will have to pass certain stages in the permanent residence process before you are eligible to receive a work permit).

Such an inland application would be made to the Inland Case Processing Centre in Vegreville, Alberta, using the form found in Schedule 9 (page 247).

7:2.3 Applying for a work permit outside Canada

If you do not fall into any of the above criteria, your application will be submitted to a visa post, using the form found in Figure 18. As noted at the beginning of this chapter, in order to qualify for a work permit you must meet the requirements for temporary residence[7], as well as the requirements for the issuing of a work permit. You do not have to apply separately for a Temporary Resident Visa (TRV) when you apply for your work permit. It is included in your work permit application.

If your application is approved, you will receive a letter confirming the approval. This letter is not your work permit. When you arrive in Canada you must show this letter to a Canadian officer at a port of entry.

[7]For more details about these requirements, see Chapter 9.

				PAGE 1 OF/DE 2

Citizenship and Immigration Canada — Citoyenneté et Immigration Canada

PROTECTED WHEN COMPLETED
PROTÉGÉ UNE FOIS REMPLI . B

APPLICATION FOR A WORK PERMIT
DEMANDE D'UN PERMIS DE TRAVAIL

I want service in: / Je veux être servi(e) en : ☐ English Anglais ☐ French Français

File - Référence

1 Surname (Family name) - Nom de famille | First name - Prénom | Middle name - Autre(s) prénom(s)

2 My current mailing address. All correspondence will go to this address. If you wish to authorize the release of information from your case file to a representative, indicate their address below and on the form IMM 5476.
Mon adresse postale actuelle. Toute la correspondance sera envoyée à cette adresse. Si vous désirez autoriser la transmission de renseignements concernant votre dossier à un représentant, indiquez son adresse ci-dessous et sur le formulaire IMM 5476.

3 My residential address (if different from your mailing address)
Mon adresse personnelle (si elle est différente de votre adresse postale)

Telephone number
Numéro de téléphone ▶

Fax number
Numéro de télécopieur ▶

4 Date of birth-Date de naissance D - J M Y - A
5 Place of birth - Lieu de naissance City/Town - Ville/Village Prov./State - Prov./État Country - Pays
6 Citizen of - Citoyenneté

7 Sex - Sexe ☐ Male Homme ☐ Female Femme
8 Present marital status - État civil ☐ Unmarried (never married) Célibataire ☐ Engaged Fiancé(e) ☐ Married Marié(e) ☐ Widowed Veuf (Veuve) ☐ Separated Séparé(e) ☐ Divorced Divorcé(e) ☐ Common law Conjoint de fait

9 Personal details of family members (spouse or common-law partner and dependent children)
Renseignements sur les membres de ma famille (conjoint(e) ou conjoint(e) de fait et enfants dépendants)

	APPLICANT REQUERANT	SPOUSE OR COMMON-LAW PARTNER AND CHILDREN ÉPOUX OU CONJOINT DE FAIT ET ENFANTS			
Family name Nom de famille					
First and second names Prénom(s)					
Relationship Lien de parenté	SELF LUI MÊME				
Date of birth Date de naissance	D - J M Y - A	D - J M Y - A	D - J M Y - A	D - J M Y - A	
Place of birth Lieu de naissance					
Citizenship Citoyenneté					
Passport no. N° de passeport					
Passport expiry date Date d'expiration du passeport	D - J M Y - A	D - J M Y - A	D - J M Y - A	D - J M Y - A	
Marital status État matrimonial					
Will accompany you to Canada? Vous accompagnera au Canada?		☐ Yes Oui ☐ No Non	☐ Yes Oui ☐ No Non	☐ Yes Oui ☐ No Non	

10

DO NOT WRITE IN THIS SPACE
ESPACE RÉSERVÉ

Officer - Agent

IMM 1295 (06-2002) B

Canadä

Fig. 18.   Application for a work permit.

PAGE 2 OF/DE 2

11 My present job is (Give your job title and a brief description of your position)
Profession actuelle (Indiquer le titre de votre emploi et une brève description du poste)

12 I have held my present job for
J'occupe mon emploi actuel depuis

Month(s) Mois

Year(s) An(s)

13 The name and address of my employer and the type of business are - Nom et adresse de mon employeur (préciser également le genre d'entreprise)

14 The name and address of my prospective employer in Canada are (Attach original offer of employment)
Nom et adresse de mon employeur éventuel au Canada (Joindre l'original de l'offre d'emploi)

15 My occupation in Canada will be (Give your job title and a brief description of your position)
Ma profession au Canada sera (Indiquer le titre de votre emploi et une brève description du poste)

16 My salary will be - Mon salaire sera de

$ Cdn $ (Canadiens)

17 I am expected to start my employment on
Je suis censé commencer à travailler le

D - J   M   Y - A

18 My employment is expected to finish on
Il est prévu que mon emploi prendra fin le

D - J   M   Y - A

19 Have you or any member of your family ever:
Les questions suivantes s'adressent également au visiteur et à tout membre de sa famille

("X" the appropriate box)
(Inscrire « X » dans la case appropriée)

a) Been treated for any serious physical or mental disorders or any communicable or chronic diseases?
Vous a-t-on jamais traité(e) pour une maladie mentale ou physique grave, ou pour une maladie contagieuse ou chronique?
☐ Yes / Oui   ☐ No / Non

b) Committed, been arrested or charged with **any** criminal offence in **any** country?
Avez-vous commis, ou avez-vous été arrêté pour avoir commis ou accusé d'avoir commis une infraction pénale quelconque dans n'**importe quel** pays?
☐ Yes / Oui   ☐ No / Non

c) Been refused admission to, or ordered to leave Canada?
Vous a-t-on jamais refusé l'admission au Canada, ou enjoint de quitter le Canada?
☐ Yes / Oui   ☐ No / Non

d) Applied for **any** Canadian Immigration visas
(e.g. Permanent Resident, Student, Worker, Temporary Resident (visitor), Temporary Resident Permit)?
Avez-vous demandé un visa canadien **auparavant?**
(par exemple, un visa de résident permanent, d'étudiant, de travailleur, de résident temporaire [visiteur] ou un permis de séjour temporaire)?
☐ Yes / Oui   ☐ No / Non

e) Been refused a visa to travel to Canada?
Vous a-t-on jamais refusé un visa pour le Canada?
☐ Yes / Oui   ☐ No / Non

f) In periods of either peace or war, have you ever been involved in the commission of a war crime or crime against humanity, such as: wilful killing, torture, attacks upon, enslavement, starvation or other inhumane acts committed against civilians or prisoners of war, or deportation of civilians?
En période de paix ou de guerre, avez-vous déjà participé à la commission d'un crime de guerre ou d'un crime contre l'humanité, c'est-à-dire de tout acte inhumain commis contre des populations civiles ou des prisonniers de guerre, par exemple, l'assassinat, la torture, l'agression, la réduction en esclavage ou la privation de nourriture, etc., ou encore participé à la déportation de civils?
☐ Yes / Oui   ☐ No / Non

If the answer to any of the above is "yes", give details - Si vous avez répondu « oui » à l'une ou l'autre question ci-dessus, veuillez préciser

20 During the past five years have you or any family member accompanying you lived in any other country than your country of citizenship or permanent residence for more than six months?
Au cours des cinq dernières années, avez-vous ou n'importe quel membre de votre famille vous accompagnant a-t-il vécu dans un autre pays que votre pays de citoyenneté ou de résidence permanente pendant plus de six mois?
☐ Yes / Oui   ☐ No / Non

21 If answer to question 20 is "yes" list countries and length of stay
Si la réponse à la question 20 est affirmative, indiquer le nom de ces pays et la durée du séjour

Name Nom	Country Pays	Length of stay - Durée du séjour	
		From - De	To - A
		D - J M Y - A	D - J M Y - A

22 I declare that I have answered all required questions in this application fully and truthfully
Je déclare avoir donné des réponses exactes et complètes à toutes les questions de la présente demande

D - J   M   Y - A

Signature of applicant - Signature du requérant

Date

IMM 1295 (06-2002) B

Fig. 18. continued.

7:3 WHAT THE APPLICATION FOR A WORK PERMIT SHOULD INCLUDE

As mentioned in Chapter 1, your application will have to include the fees, completed forms and the supporting documentation. With regard to the supporting documentation, please note that a copy of the job offer must be included with the worker's application for a work permit. It must be identical to the job offer that was sent to HRSDC, and it has to be accompanied by the HRSDC confirmation letter.

See Figure 19 for a sample Checklist of items to be included in an application for a work permit.

7:4 CONDITIONS ON THE WORK PERMIT

An officer may impose, vary or cancel conditions when issuing a work permit. These may include one or more of the following:

◆ the type of employment in which you may work;

◆ the employer for whom you may work;

◆ where you may work;

◆ how long you may continue to work.

7:5 AMENDMENTS TO/RENEWALS OF WORK PERMITS

Once in Canada, you may need to apply to change your permit if:

Citizenship and
Immigration Canada

Citoyenneté et
Immigration Canada

PAGE 1 OF 1

DOCUMENT CHECKLIST
FOR A WORK PERMIT

The documents you need to attach to your application are detailed on this form. If any of the required documents are missing, your application will be returned to you.

All documents in a language other than English or French must be translated. Provide both a photocopy of the document and the translation in English or French.

I have enclosed the following items:

Put an "X" in the box when you have enclosed the item

- Completed "**Application for a Work Permit**" (IMM 1295) ☐

- Your job offer letter or contract from your prospective employer, and the file number provided by Human Resources Development Canada (HRDC) to locate the Labour market opinion. Your employer should be able to provide you with this file identifier ☐

- Proof indicating you meet the requirements of the job being offered ☐

- If working in Quebec provide evidence of a valid "**Certificate d'acceptation du Québec**" (CAQ) ☐

- Proof of identity as specified under the "**Working in Canada**" section of this guide ☐

- Proof of funds available as specified under the "**Working in Canada**" section of this guide ☐

- Fee payment in an acceptable format. Verify acceptable methods of payment with the Visa office responsible for your area.
  Note: Visa offices cannot accept fee payments from banks in Canada ☐

- "**Statutory Declaration of Common-law Union**" (IMM 5409) (if applicable) ☐

- Any additional documents required by the responsible visa office ☐

IMM 5488 (06-2002) E

(DISPONIBLE EN FRANÇAIS - IMM 5488 F)

Canada

Fig. 19. Document checklist for a work permit.

◆ you change jobs, or

◆ you wish to work beyond the period provided in your initial work permit.

If you wish to change any condition of your work permit or you wish to renew it, you must make an application to the Inland Case Processing Centre in Vegreville, Alberta. The forms, including the applicable checklist, and accompanying guidelines can be found at **www.cic.gc.ca/english/applications/visitor.html**. For samples of the main form and Checklist, see Schedule 9 (page 247). Please note that such amendments still require meeting of relevant conditions, such as HRSDC reconfirmation.

7:6 SPECIAL PROGRAMS

Citizenship and Immigration Canada offers several programmes to facilitate the application process for work permits in industries with a greater need for skilled workers. Currently there are two such programmes in place:

◆ Facilitated Processing for Information Technology Workers;

◆ Tool and Die Machinists in Ontario.

Please note that these special programmes change. For updated information with regard to the special programmes in place at a particular time, please visit **www.cic.gc.ca**, select 'Choose Canada to Work' and further select 'The Employer's Role'.

7:7 THE LIVE-IN CAREGIVER PROGRAM

A live-in caregiver is someone who provides care to children, the elderly or the disabled in a private household. After working two years as a live-in caregiver, you can apply to be a permanent resident in Canada. To become a live-in caregiver, you must speak English or French, have a high-school diploma and have appropriate training or experience. You will still need an employer to 'sponsor' you, as with any work permit application. For more information, visit **www.cic.gc.ca/english/pub/caregiver/index.html**.

7:8 SPOUSES AND DEPENDANTS

If your family members wish to follow you to Canada at a later date, they must make a separate application for admission. It is important to know that spouses, common-law partners and dependants who accompany a foreign worker to Canada need to have their own work permit if they want to work in Canada. They may, however, apply from within Canada. And provided that you, the foreign worker, are:

a. authorised to work in Canada for six months or longer; and

b. doing a work that is listed in Skill level O, A or B in the NOC[8],

your spouse or common-law partner may apply for a work permit without having to obtain an HRSDC job confirmation. The work permit obtained by him or her will be valid for as long as the principal applicant's permit.

[8]For more information about the NOC, see Chapter 2 and Schedule 5 (page 232).

This concludes our overview of the relevant aspects of an application for a work permit. Please ensure coordination of all employer and employee aspects of an application for smooth processing.

8

Studying in Canada

8:1 THE STEPS INVOLVED IN OBTAINING A STUDY PERMIT[1]

In general, there are three stages to the process of coming to study in Canada. The first step involves research; you should become familiar with issues such as the range, cost and duration of courses/programmes that Canadian institutions offer. Below are a few helpful hints about this part of the process. The second stage is the application for admission to the institution(s) of your choice; this stage will hopefully result in one or more offers of admission. The last step is that of applying for the actual study permit to Citizenship and Immigration Canada (CIC).

8:1.1 INTRODUCTION TO POST-SECONDARY EDUCATION[2] IN CANADA

The post-secondary programmes and courses that are offered in Canada vary in duration from less than six months to five years or more. You may study to get a certificate, a

---

[1]A **study permit** is the official document issued by an officer that allows someone who is not a Canadian citizen or permanent resident to study in Canada.

[2]Education undertaken after completion of high-school. Note that student permits are also available for elementary and secondary studies, but are not covered in this book.

college diploma or a university degree (Bachelor's Degree – three/four years, Master's Degree – one or two years) or you may pursue a doctoral/PhD programme or a professional degree[3].

In Canada there are four types of institutions that offer post-secondary education:

◆ universities, offering certificate, degree or professional degree programmes;

◆ community colleges, offering college diploma as well as degree and applied degree programmes;

◆ university colleges, that have university degree, college diploma and certificate programmes;

◆ career colleges/private vocational colleges, which are privately-owned institutions that provide training for shorter periods of time.

For more information about each of these categories and the differences between the types of programmes mentioned above, please visit **www.studyincanada.com**, and select 'Canadian Education System' from the top menu.

A list with all the Canadian universities and their web sites is found below. For a list of all colleges and their internet addresses, visit the web site of the Association of Canadian Community Colleges, at **www.accc.ca**.

[3]Such as law or dentistry.

British Columbia

The University of British Columbia, Vancouver
   www.ubc.ca

British Columbia Open University, Burnaby
   www.ola.bc.ca

University College of the Cariboo, Kamloops
   www.cariboo.bc.ca

Emily Carr Institute of Art and Design, Vancouver
   www.eciad.bc.ca

University College of Fraser Valley, Abbotsford
   www.ucfv.bc.ca

Malaspina University-College, Nanaimo
   www.mala.bc.ca

University of Northern British Columbia, Prince George
   www.unbc.ca

Okanagan University College, Kelowna
   www.ouc.bc.ca

Royal Roads University, Victoria
   www.royalroads.ca

Simon Fraser University, Burnaby
   www.sfu.ca/

Trinity Western University, Langley
   www.twu.ca

University of Victoria, Victoria
   www.uvic.ca

Alberta

University of Alberta, Edmonton
   www.ualberta.ca/

Athabasca University, Athabasca
   www.athabascau.ca

Augustana University College, Camrose
www.augustana.ca
University of Calgary, Calgary
www.ucalgary.ca
Concordia University College of Alberta, Edmonton
www.concordia.ab.ca
The Kings University College, Edmonton
www.kingsu.ab.ca
The University of Lethbridge, Lethbridge
home.uleth.ca

Saskatchewan
Campion College, Regina
www.campioncollege.sk.ca
Luther College, Regina
www.luthercollege.edu
University of Regina, Regina
www.uregina.ca
University of Saskatchewan, Saskatoon
www.usask.ca
Saskatchewan Indian Federated College, Regina
www.sifc.edu
St Thomas More College, Saskatoon
www.usask.ca/stm

Manitoba
Brandon University, Brandon
www.brandonu.ca
Collège universitaire de Saint-Boniface, Saint-Boniface
www.ustboniface.mb.ca
University of Manitoba, Winnipeg
www.umanitoba.ca

University of Winnipeg, Winnipeg
www.uwinnipeg.ca

Ontario
Brescia University College, London
www.uwo.ca/brescia
Brock University, St Catharines,
www.brocku.ca
Carleton University, Ottawa
www.carleton.ca
Collège dominicain de philosophie et de théologie, Ottawa
www.collegedominicain.ca
University of Guelph, Guelph
www.uoguelph.ca
Huron University College, London
www.huronuc.on.ca
King's College, London
www.uwo.ca/kings
Lakehead University, Thunder Bay
www.lakeheadu.ca
Laurentian University of Sudbury, Sudbury
www.laurentian.ca
McMaster University, Hamilton
www.mcmaster.ca
Nipissing University, North Bay
www.nipissingu.ca
University of Ottawa, Ottawa
www.upottawa.ca
Queen's University at Kingston, Kingston
www.queensu.ca

Redeemer University College, Lancaster
www.redeemer.on.ca
Ryerson University, Toronto
www.ryerson.ca
Saint Paul University, Ottawa
www.ustpaul.ca
St Jerome's University, Waterloo
www.sju.ca
University of St Michael's College, Toronto
www.utoronto.ca/stmikes
University of Sudbury, Sudbury
www.usudbury.com
University of Toronto, Toronto
www.utoronto.ca
Trent University, Peterborough
www.trentu.ca
University of Trinity College, Toronto
www.trinity.utoronto.ca
Victoria University, Toronto
www.vicu.utoronto.ca
University of Waterloo, Waterloo
www.uwaterloo.ca
The University of Western Ontario, London
www.uwo.ca
Wilfrid Laurier University, Waterloo
www.wlu.ca
University of Windsor, Windsor
www.uwindsor.ca
York University, Toronto
www.yorku.ca

Quebec
Bishops University, Lennoxville
www.ubishops.ca
Concordia University, Montreal
www.concordia.ca
HEC Montréal, Montréal
www.hec.ca
Université Laval, Québec
www.ulaval.ca
McGill University, Montréal
www.mcgill.ca
Université de Montréal, Montréal
www.umontreal.ca
École Polytechnique de Montréal, Montréal
www.polymtl.ca
Université de Québec: École nationale d'administration
publique, Québec
www.enap.ca
Université du Québec: École de technologie supérieure,
Montréal
www.etsmtl.ca
Université du Québec: Institut national de la recherche
scientifique, Sainte-Foy
www.inrs.uquebec.ca
Université du Québec: Télé-université, Québec
www.teluq.uquebec.ca
Université du Québec à Chicoutimi, Cicoutimi
www.uqac.ca
Université du Québec à Montréal, Montréal
www.uqam.ca
Université du Québec à Rimouski, Rimouski
www.uqar.qc.ca

Université du Québec en Abitibi-Témiscamingue,
Rouyn-Noranda
www.uqat.ca
Université du Québec en Outaouais, Gatineau
www.uqo.ca
Université du Québec à Trois-Rivières, Trois-Rivières
www.uqtr.ca
Université du Québec, Québec
www.uquebec.ca
Université de Sherbrooke, Sherbrooke
www.usherbrooke.ca

Newfoundland
Memorial University of Newfoundland, St John's
www.mun.ca

New Brunswick
Université de Moncton, Moncton
www.umoncton.ca
Mount Allison University, Sackville
www.mta.ca
University of New Brunswick, Fredericton
www.unb.ca
St Thomas University, Fredericton
www.stthomasu.ca

Prince Edward Island
University of Prince Edward Island, Charlottetown
www.upei.ca

Novia Scotia

Acadia University, Wolfville
www.acadiau.ca
University College of Cape Breton, Sydney
www.uccb.ns.ca
Dalhousie University, Halifax
www.dal.ca
University of King's College, Halifax
www.ukings.ns.ca
Mount Saint Vincent University, Halifax
www.msvu.ca
Nova Scotia Agricultural College, Truro
www.nsac.ns.ca
Novia Scotia College of Art and Design, Halifax
www.nscad.ns.ca
Université Sainte-Anne, Pointe-de-l'Église
www.ustanne.ednet.ns.ca
St Francis Xavier University, Antigonish
www.stfx.ca
Saint Mary's University, Halifax
www.stmarys.ca

For a summary of relevant information with regard to each institution mentioned above, visit the site of the Association of Canadian Community Colleges at **www.aucc.ca**, select 'Canadian Universities' from the right side of the page and then select 'Our Universities' from the left side of the following page.

8:2 THE RESEARCH

If you are seriously considering the option of completing post-secondary studies in Canada, you should start your research more than a year in advance of the date you would like to begin. Usually, entry points for international students are the September and January semesters. It is best to start early because each institution has its own deadline for accepting applications, and the deadline may be as early as ten months in advance of the beginning of studies.

In terms of sources of information, the course calendars that most institutions post online are a good place to start. In addition, you may wish to contact the registrar/admissions offices of the institutions you are interested in, and request that they mail you their information packages. You can also search for specific programmes and the institutions that offer them at **www.studyincanada.com/english/sinfo/index.asp**.

Listed below are the sources of information regarding studies in Canada.

University programmes

Association of Universities and Colleges of Canada
600-350 Albert Street, Ottawa,
Ontario, K1R 1B1, Canada
Tel: (613) 563-1236, Fax: (613) 563-9745
www.aucc.ca/

College programmes

Association of Canadian Community Colleges
#200-1223 Michael Street North, Gloucester,
Ontario, K1J 7T2, Canada
Tel: (613) 746-2222, Fax (613) 746-6721
www.accc.ca/

Private career college programmes

National Association of Career Colleges
#403-233 Colbourne Street, P.O. Box 340, Brantford,
Ontario, N3T 5N3, Canada
Tel: (519) 753-8689, Fax: (519) 753-4712
www.nacc.ca/

Studying in Canada

Canadian Bureau for International Education
220 Laurier Avenue West, Suite 1100, Ottawa,
Ontario, K1P 5Z9, Canada
Tel: (613) 237-4820, Fax: (613) 237-1073
www.cbie.ca/

French and English second language programmes

Council of Second Language Programs in Canada
P.O. Box 53063, Ottawa,
Ontario, K1N 1C5, Canada
E-mail: **info@cslp.com   www.cslp.com**

Distance education

Canada:
www.educationcanada.cmec.ca/EN/Distance.stm
Provinces and Territories:
www.educationcanada.cmec.ca/EN/Maps/MapDistance.stm

8:2.1 Things to look for

In doing your research, you may want to pay particular attention to admission requirements, entry dates, programme length and costs.

Each Canadian institution sets its **own admission requirements** and selects applicants who meet those requirements. You should contact the institution(s) to which you intend to apply. For an overview of general admission standards, visit **www.studyincanada.com**, select 'Choosing a School' and then select 'General Requirements'.

You should note that engineering, optometry, medicine, veterinary medicine, law, and dentistry are fields for which there is a great deal of academic competition for admission and most universities have limits or quotas on the number of qualified applicants admitted each year. A high level of academic achievement is required for admission. Often, at least two years of university studies, sometimes in a related field, are required before you can be admitted to study in these fields. On top of that, you may be required to take a test, such as LSAT (law) or DAT (dentistry) before you can be considered for admission into such courses of studies.

It is important to take into account the language requirements. You do not have to speak both English and French to study at a Canadian university – however, you will have to show proficiency in one, depending on the university where you apply. Most English universities require a score of 560 or better on the Test of English as a Foreign Language (TOEFL). Canadian French-language universities usually assess applicants on a case-by-case basis. See Schedule 6 (page 242) for the web site addresses of language tests providers.

The particular costs that you should be looking for in your research are:

◆ admission fees;

◆ tuition fees (for international/visa students);

◆ housing;

◆ food expenses;

◆ books and supplies;

◆ personal living expenses (transportation, entertainment);

◆ health insurance.

8:3 APPLYING FOR ADMISSION

An application usually includes forms and supporting documentation. The information packages sent by the institution(s) will most likely include:

a. hard copies of the forms to be filled in and submitted; and also

b. a list of the supporting documents that must be provided, for example, proof of having completed high school.

You should be able to find and print these materials (forms and list of documents) online, on the individual web sites of the university/college. In addition, in some provinces admission applications can be submitted electronically, in

which case you will only have to mail the supporting documents. For more information about electronic applications,
visit the following sites:

◆ **Alberta**: Alberta Learning Information Service –
Electronic Application Service: **www.alis.gov.ab.ca/
learning/ao/postsecondary.asp**

◆ **British Columbia**: Post-Secondary Application Service of
British Columbia: **www.pas.bc.ca/**

◆ **Ontario**: Ontario Universities Application Centre:
www.ouac.on.ca/
Ontario College Application Service: **www.ocas.on.ca**

◆ **Quebec**: Montreal region: **www.sram.qc.ca/**
Quebec City region: **www.sraq.qc.ca/**
Saguenay/Lac St-Jean region: **www.sras.qc.ca/**

In terms of mailing your admission application package, you
may consider sending it by courier or registered mail, in
order to avoid potential delays resulting from it being lost if
sent by regular mail. Once your application is received, the
institution(s) to which you have applied will send you a letter
of confirmation. If you do not receive such a letter within a
few weeks of having sent your package, you should contact
the admissions/registrar office(s) and inquire about your
application.

Some institutions may provide you with a way to check the
status of your application online. You should monitor
the status of your application, either online or by being in
touch with the admissions/registrar office, and you should

not hesitate to contact the university/college if you have any concerns relating to it.

8:3.1 The letter of admission

The institution(s) to which you have applied for admission will usually take a decision with regard to your application within four to six months of the deadline for submission. However, please note that the time frame for an answer may vary from one university or college to another.

If an institution is willing to offer you admission, they will send you a letter that contains such an offer. Please be aware that in order to be considered 'admitted', you need to write back and formally accept the offer, usually by a certain date that is mentioned in the offer of admission.

The university/college should provide you with a letter you will need in order to apply for a study permit. See Figure 20 for guidelines and sample letter of acceptance as provided by CIC.

8:4 APPLYING FOR A STUDY PERMIT

8:4.1 When a study permit is not necessary

There are certain courses of study for which a study permit is not required:

◆ a course/programme that is less than six months in duration;

STUDENT INFORMATION

1. Family name: 2. First name and initials:

3. Date of birth: 4. Student 10 number:

5. Student's full mailing address: 6. Dates:

Start date: Day -Month -Year - Completion date: Day -Month -
Year - or minimum --years of full-time studies

7. Name of schooVinstitution (indicate private or public): 8. Levr.l of study:

9. Program/Major/Course: 1*.DFull- Time 0 Part- Time

Hours of instruction/week:-

11. Academic year of study which the student will enter 12. Late registration date:
(e.g., Vear 2 of 3-year program):
Day -Month -Year -

13. Condition of acceptance specified as clearly as possible 14. Estimated tuition fee for this course:
(e.g., TOEFL, partial fee payment):

15. Scholarship/Teaching assistantship: 16. Exchange student:

DVes DNo

17. Licensing information where applicable for private institution: 18. If destined to Quebec, has CAQ information been sent to student?: DVes DNo DN/A DVes

DNo DN/A

19. Guardianship/Custodianship details if applicable: 20. Intemship/Work practicum:

DVes DNo

If yes, length of intemship/work practicum:

21 Other relevant information:

22. Signature of institution representative (e.g., Registrar):

23. Name of institution representative (please print):

Fig. 20.   Guidelines and sample letter of acceptance from CIC.

Letter of Acceptance

Background

After consultation with stakeholders, Citizenship and Immigration Canada has produced a standardized letter of acceptance to be filled out by educational institutions. Completing the letter of acceptance correctly will facilitate the initial processing of the student's application at missions abroad and ports of entry as well as future applications for extensions of study permits in Canada.

As changes to this form may need to be made in the future, institutions with computer-generated registration systems may wish to wait a while before reprogramming their computer systems to include this letter.

Completion of form

The letter of acceptance from the institution must include the institution's letterhead, full mailing address, telephone and fax numbers, and e-mail and Web site addresses if applicable.

Some information may not be applicable or may not be known at the time of application. If the information is not applicable, please indicate N/A. If the information is not known, indicate N/K.

The following are guidelines for information requested in the letter of acceptance:

1. & 2. Family name, First name and initials: Full name of student as shown in the student's identity document (e.g., passport/travel documents, birth certificate, alien resident card or nationalID card).

5. Student's full mailing address: Street, P.O. Box, City, Country and Postal Code.

7. Name of school/institution: The letter of acceptance from the institution must include the institution's full mailing address, telephone and fax numbers, e-mail and Web site addresses and name of contact, if not already included in your letterhead.

   In cases where the program is jointly offered by more than one institution, the letter of acceptance should be issued by the institution that will be granting the degree or diploma (or, where a degree or diploma is granted jointly by more than one institution, the letter of acceptance should be issued by the institution at which students will begin their studies). The letter should note that the program of study includes courses/sessions (specify which semesters/courses) given at another institution (specify institution name, type fie. College, university, technical institute, etc] , and location).

8. Level of study: Level refers to primary, secondary, trade, post-secondary, Bachelor's degree, Master's degree, Doctorate degree, other university studies, other studies and interns and residents.

9. Program/Major/Course: Examples include ESL, FSL, Science, Secretarial and Pilot.

12. Late registration date: This refers to students who are unable to arrive in Canada prior to the normal registration date.

14. Estimated tuition fee for this course: Total fees required, including tuition and homestay/ boarding if applicable. You should also indicate whether fees were prepaid by applicant.

17. Licensing information where applicable for private institution: Is the institution private? (Yes or no).

18. CAQ is the Quebec Certificate of Acceptance.

21. Other relevant information: This space is provided to allow you to add any relevant information to assist the visa office in making a decision.

Fig. 20. continued.

◆ courses that are not academic, professional or vocational in nature.

In such cases, although you may not need a study permit to complete your studies, you must nevertheless ensure that your stay does not extend past the time specified by the immigration authorities upon entry in Canada. If you anticipate that that will be the case, prepare an application to extend your stay in Canada and submit it at least 30 days before the end of the six months. For more details, see section 8:6 below.

If you come to Canada for a short programme and you are planning to continue your studies in another programme after the short programme, you are encouraged to apply for a study permit before you come to Canada. This will allow you to apply for your new programme from within Canada. Otherwise, you will have to apply to a Canadian visa office abroad.

8:4.2 General requirements for a study permit

In order to obtain a study permit, you will have to:

◆ provide a letter of acceptance from the educational institution you plan to attend;

◆ prove that you have enough money to pay school fees and support yourself and your family, if applicable;

◆ take a medical exam in some cases;

◆ qualify as a temporary resident in Canada, including a temporary resident visa if needed; for more details about the requirements associated with these, see Chapter 9; and

◆ satisfy an officer that you will leave Canada at the end of your studies.

8:4.3 Specific requirements

As mentioned in Chapter 1, to find out exactly what documents you need to include in your study permit application, you must contact the relevant visa office. See Schedule 1 (page 219) to determine which office you should contact, and also visit the site of Citizenship and Immigration Canada at **www.cic.gc.ca** for up-to-date information.

8:4.4 Supporting documents

In general, the supporting documents that you will have to provide are the following:

◆ proof of identity (a valid passport or travel document that guarantees re-entry to the country that issued it);

◆ proof of acceptance from an educational institution (the letter provided by the institution); and

◆ proof of funds that are sufficient to cover your and, if applicable, your family's living expenses while in Canada (e.g. bank statement or proof of payment of tuition and residence fees).

For more information, please consult the study permit application guidelines, that can be obtained as specified in Chapter 1. For a sample application, see Figure 21.

Fig. 21. Application for a study permit.

PAGE 2 OF/DE 2

7 I have been accepted at the following educational institution (attach original letter of acceptance)
J'ai été accepté à l'établissement d'enseignement suivant (joindre l'original de la lettre d'acceptation)

Name of school
Nom de l'établissement d'enseignement

Complete address of school in Canada
Indiquer l'adresse au complet de cet établissement au Canada

8 My program of study and level will be
Mon programme d'études

9 My program of study will begin
Mon programme d'études commencera
D - J   M   Y - A

My program of study will end
Mon programme d'études se terminera
D - J   M   Y - A

10 The cost of my studies will be (in Canadian dollars)
Coût de mes études (en dollars canadiens)

Tuition
Frais de scolarité $

Room and board
Pension $

Other
Autre $

11 Funds available for my stay in Canada
Je dispose, pour mon séjour au Canada, de

CDN $
$ CAN

My expenses in Canada will be paid by
Mes dépenses au Canada seront assumées par

☐ Myself or my parents
Moi-même ou mes parents

☐ Other (provide details below)
D'autre (préciser ci-dessous)

12 Have you or any member of your family ever:
Les questions suivantes s'adressent également au visiteur et à tout membre de sa famille :

"X" THE APPROPRIATE BOX
INSCRIRE « X » DANS LA CASE APPROPRIÉE

a) Been treated for any serious physical or mental disorders or any communicable or chronic diseases?
Vous a-t-on jamais traité(e) pour une maladie mentale ou physique grave, ou pour une maladie contagieuse ou chronique?

☐ YES ☐ NO
OUI   NON

b) Committed, been arrested or charged with any criminal offence in any country?
Avez-vous commis, ou avez-vous été arrêté pour avoir commis ou accusé d'avoir commis une infraction pénale quelconque dans n'importe quel pays?

☐ YES ☐ NO
OUI   NON

c) Been refused admission to, or ordered to leave Canada?
Vous a-t-on jamais refusé l'admission au Canada, ou enjoint de quitter le Canada?

☐ YES ☐ NO
OUI   NON

d) Applied for any Canadian immigration visas
(e.g. Permanent Resident, Student, Worker, Temporary Resident (visitor), Temporary Resident Permit)?
Avez-vous demandé un visa canadien auparavant?
(par exemple, un visa de résident permanent, d'étudiant, de travailleur, de résident temporaire [visiteur] ou un permis de séjour temporaire)?

☐ YES ☐ NO
OUI   NON

e) Been refused a visa to travel to Canada?
Vous a-t-on jamais refusé un visa pour le Canada?

☐ YES ☐ NO
OUI   NON

f) In periods of either peace or war, have you ever been involved in the commission of a war crime or crime against humanity, such as: willful killing, torture, attacks upon, enslavement, starvation or other inhumane acts committed against civilians or prisoners of war; or deportation of civilians?
En période de paix ou de guerre, avez-vous déjà participé à la commission d'un crime de guerre ou d'un crime contre l'humanité, c'est-à-dire de tout acte inhumain commis contre des populations civiles ou des prisonniers de guerre, par exemple, l'assassinat, la torture, l'agression, la réduction en esclavage ou la privation de nourriture, etc., ou encore participé à la déportation de civils?

☐ YES ☐ NO
OUI   NON

If the answer to any of the above is "yes", give details - Si vous avez répondu « oui » à l'une ou l'autre question ci-dessus, veuillez préciser

13 During the past five years have you or any family member accompanying you lived in any other country than your country of citizenship or permanent residence for more than six months?
Au cours des cinq dernières années, avez-vous ou n'importe quel membre de votre famille vous accompagnant a-t-il vécu dans un autre pays que votre pays de citoyenneté ou de résidence permanente pendant plus de six mois?
If answer to question 13 is "yes", list countries and length of stay
Si la réponse à la case 13 est affirmative, indiquer le nom de ces pays et la durée du séjour

☐ YES ☐ NO
OUI   NON

Name Nom	Country Pays	Length of stay - Durée du séjour	
		From - De D-J M Y-A	To - À D-J M Y-A

14 I declare that I have answered all required questions in this application fully and truthfully.
Je déclare avoir donné des réponses exactes et complètes à toutes les questions de la présente demande.

Signature of applicant - Signature du requérant

D-J M Y-A

Date

This form has been established by the Minister of Citizenship and Immigration
Formulaire établi par le ministre de la Citoyenneté et de l'Immigration

The information you provide on this form is collected under the authority of the Immigration and Refugee Protection Act to determine if you may be admitted to Canada as a student. It will be stored in Personal Information Bank CIC PPU 061, Foreign Student Records and Case File. It is protected and accessible under the Privacy Act and the Access to Information Act.

IMM 1294 (06-2002) B

Les renseignements fournis sur ce formulaire sont recueillis en vertu de la Loi sur l'immigration et la protection des réfugiés pour établir si vous êtes admissible au Canada à titre d'étudiant. Ils seront versés au fichier de renseignements personnels CIC PPU 051, Dossier et fichier des étudiants étrangers. Ils sont protégés et accessibles en vertu de la Loi sur la protection des renseignements personnels et de la Loi sur l'accès à l'information.

Fig. 21. continued.

8:5 THE STUDY PERMIT

If your application for a study permit is accepted, you will get an introduction letter from the visa office where you applied. You will also be issued a visa to come to Canada. When you enter the country, show the introduction letter from the visa office to immigration officials who will issue your study permit at the port of entry.

The conditions on your permit may tell you:

◆ how long you can stay, the date by which you must leave Canada;

◆ the types of studies or courses you may take;

◆ the educational institution you may attend;

◆ where you can study, the location of your studies;

◆ if you need to report for medical examination or observation;

◆ if you need to report to provide evidence of compliance for certain conditions;

◆ if you are permitted to work on-campus at your institution.

8:6 AMENDMENTS TO/RENEWALS OF STUDY PERMITS

Once in Canada, you may be able to change the conditions of your permit or apply to renew it. For that you will need to submit an Application to Change Conditions or Extend Your Stay in Canada, which will not be discussed in detail in this book. The application will have to be sent to the Inland

Case Processing Centre in Vegreville, Alberta. For a sample application form, see Schedule 9 (page 247).

8:7 WORKING WHILE YOU ARE STUDYING IN CANADA

As a student, you may be able to work in certain situations. However, it is advisable that you come to Canada with enough money to cover all your expenses while you are studying.

Foreign students enrolled full-time at a publicly-funded post-secondary or degree-granting institution are automatically authorised to work (up to ten hours a week) on the campus of the institution at which they are studying. They are also allowed to work at a job that is related to their studies for up to one year after graduation. In the former case, the student does not need to apply for a work permit. In the latter case, please see Chapter 7, i.e. inland work permit applications (without HRSDC confirmation).

8:8 SPOUSES AND DEPENDANTS OF STUDENTS AT CANADIAN INSTITUTIONS

Your family members can come with you to Canada. They too will have to meet all the requirements for temporary residents in Canada. For more details about this aspect, see Chapter 9.

Spouses and common-law partners of:

◆ full-time students; and

◆ former full-time students doing post-graduation employment; and

◆ post-doctoral fellows

are eligible for open or open/restricted employment authorisations, depending on the medical requirements having been met. In such cases, HRSDC confirmation is not required. For more details about the process of obtaining a work permit in general, see Chapter 7.

9

Visiting Canada

9:1 GENERAL ADMISSIBILITY REQUIREMENTS

If you seek to work in Canada (see Chapter 7) or study in Canada (see Chapter 8) or if you wish to come to Canada for a shorter period of time, for example as a tourist or on business, you must satisfy a number of requirements. To be admissible into Canada you must:

- persuade an officer that you will leave Canada when the time validated for your stay in Canada expires, i.e. that your stay will be temporary;

- show that you have the funds necessary to support yourself and your family while in Canada, and to return home;

- not intend to work[1] or study[2] in Canada unless authorised to do so;

- be law abiding and have no record of criminal activity (you may be asked to provide a Police Clearance Certificate);

[1]See Chapter 7, Fig. 16, for a list of those who while in Canada on a TRV – Temporary Resident Visa are nevertheless allowed to work without a work permit.
[2]Please note that if you are in Canada on a TRV, you may engage in a course of study provided that your study period is not longer than six months. For more details about studying in Canada, see Chapter 8.

171

◆ not be a risk to the safety or security of Canada;

◆ produce any additional documents requested by the officer to establish your admissibility;

◆ be in good health (complete a medical examination, if required).

9:2 THE TEMPORARY RESIDENT VISA (TRV)

To visit Canada, you may have to apply for a TRV at a visa post abroad. For a list of countries whose citizens require a visa to come to Canada, see Schedule 2 (page 225). As for those who do not need a visa for coming to Canada (see Schedule 3, page 227), it should be noted that they must still meet the requirements for admissibility listed in section 9:1 above.

A TRV is a document issued to you and placed in your passport by a visa office abroad. It shows that that you have met the requirements for admission in Canada as a temporary resident. Visitors, international students and foreign workers in Canada are examples of temporary residents who need to obtain a TRV before coming to Canada.[3]

A valid TRV is not a guarantee of entry into Canada. An officer at a port of entry into the country may deny you admission if you no longer meet the requirements, for example if there has been a change in circumstances between

---

[3]In addition to applying for a TRV, an international student will also have to apply for a study permit, and a foreign worker for a work permit. For more details about study and work permits, see Chapters 7 and 8.

the time you applied for the TRV and the time of your arrival in Canada.

9:2.1 Types of TRV

A TRV may be for a single entry, for multiple entries, or for transit purposes.

A **single entry** TRV allows you to enter Canada only once. However, this visa may also be used for repeated entries into Canada from the USA or St Pierre and Miquelon. Such entries must occur during the time you are authorised to stay in Canada, which may be, for example, six months from your first entry on the basis of the visa.

A **multiple entry** TRV allows you to enter Canada from any country multiple times during the validity of the visa.

A **transit** TRV is required for travel through Canada to another country by those persons who need a TRV and whose flight will stop in Canada for less than 48 hours. To obtain a transit TRV you must provide specific evidence of your travel arrangements from your transportation company or travel agent. Please note that to apply for a transit TRV, you may be asked to show your travel tickets as part of the evidence of your travel arrangements.

9:2.2 Applying for a TRV

9:2.2(a) When to apply for it
You should apply for a visa at least one month before your intended departure date. It is important to note that some factors may extend considerably the time necessary for

---

Citizenship and   Citoyenneté et
Immigration Canada   Immigration Canada

DOCUMENT CHECKLIST
FOR A TEMPORARY RESIDENT VISA

The documents you need to attach to your application are detailed on this form. If any of the required documents are missing, your application will be returned to you.

All documents in a language other than English or French must be translated. Provide both a photocopy of the document and the translation in English or French.

I have enclosed the following items:

Put an "X" in the box when you have enclosed the item

- Completed "**Application for a Temporary Resident Visa**" (IMM 5257) ☐
- Fee payment in an acceptable format. Verify acceptable methods of payment with the Visa office responsible for your area. ☐
  Note: Visa offices cannot accept payment receipts from banks in Canada.
- "**Statutory Declaration of Common-law Union**" (IMM 5409) (if applicable) ☐

For yourself and each accompanying family member included on the application:

- **Valid passport** (there must be one completely blank page other than the last page, available in each passport) ☐
- Two (2) passport sized photographs ☐
- **Photocopy** of your current immigration document (if applicable) ☐
  (e.g. study permit, work permit or temporary resident permit)
- Proof of financial support, as specified in the "**Visiting Canada**" section of this guide ☐
- **Photocopy** of your valid return ticket (if you have one) ☐
- Any additional documents required by the responsible visa office ☐

Fig. 22.   Sample checklist for a TRV application.

the processing of your application: the time it takes for the application to be delivered by post, additional requirements for certain applicants, like for example a medical exam. This is why you should check with the relevant visa office well in advance of your intended departure date, and find out exactly what are the requirements applicable to you.

9:2.2(b) What your application for a TRV will typically include

For a sample Checklist of the forms and supporting documents that you would include in a TRV application, please see Figure 22. As noted in the introduction to this book, there may be additional requirements that are specific to the visa office where you would apply.

Please note that if you intend to study or work in Canada during your visit, you must include full details of the proposed work or study in your application. For more information about studying and working in Canada, see Chapters 7 and 8.

9:3 ARRIVING IN CANADA AND EXTENDING YOUR STAY

Upon arrival at a Canadian port of entry, a customs officer will determine whether you are admissible to Canada and how long you may stay. The stamp that will be placed in your passport is valid for six months unless otherwise amended by the officer. You must leave Canada by the date specified; if you want to extend your stay, you must make an application to the Inland Case Processing Centre in Vegreville, Alberta at least a month in advance. The forms, including the applicable Checklist, and accompanying guidelines can be found at

www.cic.gc.ca/english/applications/visitor.html. For samples of the main form and Checklist, see Schedule 9 (page 247).

9:4 IMPORTANT INFORMATION REGARDING CHILDREN TRAVELLING TO CANADA

Children younger than 16 years old who are travelling alone must have information on the person who will be responsible for them. If the child is the subject of a custody order, proof of custody and the other parent's consent must also be provided. Minors travelling without their parents require a letter of permission to travel, from the non-accompanying parent(s) and a letter from their custodian in Canada.

9:5 ABOUT YOUR SPOUSE, COMMON-LAW PARTNER OR DEPENDANTS ACCOMPANYING YOU TO CANADA

Your spouse or common-law partner and dependants who wish to visit Canada must apply for permission to do so. As long as you all apply together it will not be necessary for each person to fill out separate application forms. Children 18 years and over must complete their own application form.

Your spouse or common-law partner and dependants must meet the requirements for temporary residents to Canada that were mentioned in section 9:1. It is important to note that you may be required to provide a marriage certificate and birth certificates for any accompanying family members. If you are in a common-law relationship and your common-law partner will accompany you to Canada, you will have to complete the Statutory Declaration of Common-Law Union.

9:6 USEFUL INFORMATION RELATING TO VISITING CANADA: HEALTH INSURANCE AND TAX REFUNDS

Before you come to Canada you should ensure that you have health insurance, as hospitalisation or medical services for visitors are not covered by Canada. Your travel agent should be able to suggest insurance providers.

As a visitor to Canada, you can claim a refund for the 7% goods and services tax (GST) and the 15% (Newfoundland, Nova Scotia and New Brunswick) harmonized sales tax (HST) you paid on eligible goods[4] and/or short-term accommodation[5] while visiting Canada.

As a visitor you would qualify for a tax refund if the following conditions are met:

♦ you are not a resident of Canada (for tax purposes);

♦ you purchased eligible goods, short-term accommodation or both;

♦ you paid GST/HST on these purchases;

♦ you have original receipts;

♦ the total of your purchase amounts (before taxes) for eligible goods and accommodation is at least CDN$200;

♦ each individual receipt for eligible goods shows a minimum total purchase amount (before taxes) of CDN$50;

[4]Eligible goods are tangible goods that will be taken from Canada within 60 days of purchase. Examples of purchases that do not qualify: alcohol and tobacco, car rentals, lift tickets and theatre tickets, restaurant meals, dry cleaning, parking.
[5]For stays shorter than 30 days.

◆ the goods are removed from Canada within 60 days of the date they were purchased.

If you have doubts as to whether your purchases qualify, submit all original receipts and leave it to the office to decide.

To claim a refund by mail, you need to do the following:

◆ have the good receipts stamped by Canada Customs upon departure; if you are claiming for accomodation only, you do not need to have the receipt validated;

◆ complete and sign the EH-77 form (it can be downloaded from the Canada Customs and Revenue Agency site at **www.ccra-adrc.gc.ca**);

◆ include only original receipts;

◆ include original boarding pass or ticket, if you have returned home by a commercial airliner including air, non-charter bus or ferry;

◆ mail your tax refund claim from outside Canada.

For an instant refund at a refund location, you will have to do the following:

◆ complete and sign the EH-77 form (the refund office will provide you with a copy);

◆ provide only original receipts, provide two pieces of ID – one must be a photo ID and the other must have your name and address on it;

- provide a credit card (Visa, Master Card, American Express);

- provide a plane, bus or ferry ticket (if departing Canada by private vehicle or charter bus the mail-in programme must be used);

- all good purchased must be made available for viewing.

For more information about this topic, including refunds for which non-resident business are eligible, visit the site of Canada Customs and Revenue Agency at **www.ccra-adrc.gc.ca**.

10

Other Issues Relevant to All Applications

10:1 MEDICAL CHECKS

As part of the application process of coming to Canada, you and your family members may be required to undergo a medical check. If a medical examination is required, an officer will inform you of that and will also provide you with instructions on how to proceed. This phase of the process may add over three months to the processing of your application. Please note that the health assessment has to be done by one of the doctors from the Designated Medical Practitioners list.[1]

10:1.1 Medical checks for permanent residence applicants

All applicants for permanent residence in Canada are required to have a medical check-up done. The applicant and his or her family members, whether or not accompanying the main applicant to Canada, must take and pass the medical test in order to come to Canada.

---

[1]The list is available online at **www.cic.gc.ca**. You will have to pay a fee for the medical examination.

Instructions on how to take the medical examination are sent to you after you submit your application to the visa office. The results of the examination are valid for only 12 months; if you are not admitted to Canada as a permanent resident within this time, you will be required to undergo another examination.

The doctor will not tell you the results of the check-up; however, s/he will let you know if you have a health-related problem. The designated doctor does not make the final decision with regard to whether or not a person passes the medical examination for immigration purposes; it is Citizenship and Immigration Canada (CIC) which takes the final decision on this issue.

Applications for permanent residence will not be accepted by CIC if the person's health:

◆ poses a danger to public health or safety;

◆ would cause excessive demand on health or social services in Canada. Examples of excessive demand include ongoing hospitalisation or institutional care for a physical or mental illness, and special education or training that may be required by the individual. In essence, individuals may be denied admission to Canada due to the high costs of their care.

The visa office will notify you in writing if there is a problem with your medical examination.

10:1.2 Medical checks for temporary residence applicants

If your stay in Canada as a tourist, student or temporary foreign worker will be less than six months long, in general you will not have to undergo a medical examination. If, however, your stay will extend beyond six months, you will have to get a medical check-up if you have resided in a designated country/territory[2] in the year immediately preceding the date you are seeking entry into Canada.

Some **temporary workers** are required to undergo the examination regardless of the duration of their stay in Canada. That will be the case if you intend to work in an occupation in which protection of the public health is essential. Such occupations are those that would bring you in close contact (more than three hours per day and/or risk of exchange of body fluids) with people, namely:

◆ workers in the health sciences field, including staff and employees, clinical laboratory workers, patient attendants in nursing and geriatric homes, medical students admitted to Canada to attend university, medical electives and physicians on short-term positions;

◆ teachers of primary or secondary schools or other teachers of small children;

◆ domestics;

◆ workers who give in-home care to children, the elderly and the disabled; and

◆ day nursery employees.

[2]For a list of the countries/territories, visit the site of CIC at **www.cic.gc.ca**.

Agricultural workers from some countries/territories are also required to undergo the medical exam.[3]

10:2 SECURITY CHECKS

You and all your family members who are 18 or older will be the subject of a background check. Your family members will undergo the background check whether or not they will be accompanying you to Canada. To be admissible to Canada, you and your family members must not present any risk to Canada.

Background checks are intended to bar entry into Canada of those who may disrupt law and order, threaten the country's safety and security or be detrimental to national interests. Normally, CIC establishes the admissibility of applicants for permanent residence and their family members through documents such as the immigration application form, police certificates and background records and assessments.

10:2.1 Police certificates

An applicant and his/her family members who are 18 at the time the application is made, must obtain police certificates from the countries listed in Figure 23[4], provided that they have lived in any of those countries for six months or more since reaching the age of 18.

---

[3]For a list of the countries/territories, visit the site of CIC at **www.cic.gc.ca**.
[4]For an updated list, please visit the site of CIC at **www.cic.gc.ca**.

Algeria	Guyana	Philippines
Anguilla	Honduras	Portugal
Antigua and Barbuda	Hong Kong	St Kitts and Nevis
Australia	Iceland	St Lucia
Bahamas	Indonesia	Seychelles
Bangladesh	Ireland, Republic of	Singapore
Barbados	Israel	South Africa
Belgium	Italy	Spain
Belize	Jamaica	Sri Lanka
Botswana	Japan	Surinam
British Virgin Islands	Jordan (West Bank only)	Swaziland
Brunei	Kenya	Sweden
Cambodia	Lesotho	Switzerland
Cayman Islands	Luxembourg	Syria
Costa Rica	Macao	Taiwan
Cyprus	Malawi	Tanzania
Denmark	Malaysia	Trinidad and Tobago
Dominica	Malta	Tunisia
El Salvador	Mauritius	Turkey
Fiji	Mayotte	Turks and Caicos Is.
Finland	Montserrat	United Kingdom
France	Morocco	United States*
French Guyana	Myanmar	Vietnam
French Polynesia	New Zealand	Yugoslavia
Gambia	Namibia	Zambia
Germany	Nigeria	Zimbabwe
Ghana	Norway	
Greece	Pakistan	

*If you have lived in the United States, you must provide a state certificate *and* a national FBI certificate

Fig. 23. Countries from which a police certificate is required.

The police certificates that must be submitted with the application have to:

◆ be originals;

◆ be issued within the three months immediately preceding the date of making the application; and

◆ indicate either any criminal record or the absence of a criminal record.

It is your responsibility to contact the relevant authorities[5] from the countries from which you must obtain a police clearance. Embassies or consulates of the countries concerned may be able to give you additional information with regard to the process.

You may have to provide information or documentation such as photographs, authorisation to release personal information, fingerprints, or your addresses and periods of residence in other countries. Some authorities may require a letter from CIC confirming that you have applied to immigrate to Canada and that you must obtain evidence of any criminal record as part of the processing of your application.

10:2.2 Additional information required for security purposes

If you have lived in one of the countries listed in the table below,[6] additional supplementary forms will have to be included in your application. Contact the relevant visa office for more information.

Argentina	Japan	Sri Lanka
Egypt	Republic of Ireland	Switzerland
Germany	South Korea	United States*
Israel		

*Only if you have served in the U.S. military

---

[5]They may be the police or municipal, provincial, federal or similar governmental authorities.
[6]For an updated list, visit the site of CIC at **www.cic.gc.ca**.

10:2.3 What happens if you have a criminal record

Generally, persons with a criminal conviction are not admitted into Canada. However, if a prescribed period has passed after they have completed their sentence or committed an offence and during which they were not convicted of a subsequent offence, they may be deemed to have been rehabilitated. Please find below more information about this topic.

If you or any of your family members have committed a criminal offence, you must provide, in addition to any police certificates or clearances, a full description of the circumstances surrounding the offence and the court record.

10:2.3.a Criminal record abroad
If you were convicted of, or committed a criminal offence outside Canada, you may be deemed to have been rehabilitated if:

◆ ten years have passed since you have completed the sentence imposed or since you have committed the offence; and

◆ the offence is one that would, in Canada, be an indictable offence punishable by a maximum term of imprisonment of less than ten years.

If the offence is one that would, in Canada, be prosecuted summarily and if you were convicted of two or more such offences, that period is five years after the sentence imposed was served or to be served.

For a table with more information about the classification of offences in Canada and the length of rehabilitation periods, please see Figure 24.

| | Rehabilitation period | |
Conviction or offence	When deemed rehabilitated[1]	When eligible to apply for rehabilitation[2]
Conviction of an offence outside Canada that, if committed in Canada, would be an indictable offence punishable by a maximum term of imprisonment of less than 10 years	At least 10 years after completion of sentence imposed	Five years after completion of sentence imposed
Commission of an offence outside Canada that, if committed in Canada, would be an indictable offence punishable by a maximum term of imprisonment of less than 10 years	At least 10 years after commission of the offence	Five years after commission of the offence
Conviction or commission of an offence outside Canada, that, if committed in Canada, would be punishable by a maximum term of imprisonment of 10 years or more	Not applicable	Five years from completion of the sentence or commission of the offence
Two or more summary conviction offences committed outside Canada	Five years after the sentence imposed is served or to be served	Not applicable

Fig. 24. Types of offences and length of rehabilitation periods.

1The person must not have committed or been convicted of a subsequent offence.
2The person must not have committed or been convicted of a subsequent offence.

10:2.3.b Criminal record in Canada

If you have a criminal conviction in Canada, you must seek a pardon from the National Parole Board of Canada before you apply for immigration to Canada. For further information, contact:

Clemency and Pardons Division
National Parole Board
410 Laurier Avenue West
Ottawa ON K1A 0R1
Tel: 1-800-874-2652 (callers in Canada and the
    United States only)
Fax: 1-613-941-4981
www.npb-cnlc.gc.ca (the guide which includes
    application forms can be downloaded from the website)

If you have had two or more summary convictions in Canada, you may be deemed rehabilitated and no longer inadmissible if:

◆ five years have passed since the sentence imposed was served or to be served;

◆ you have had no subsequent convictions; and

◆ you have not been refused a pardon.

10:2.3.c Additional option for overcoming inadmissibility

In the event that none of the methods discussed are available to resolve inadmissibility into Canada (due to the existence of a criminal record) you may apply for a temporary resident permit, or in some cases 'rehabilitation' (a permanent removal of the immigration barrier) if enough time has passed. In such an application, you will need to convince an officer that the reason for your coming to Canada is valid, and that there no longer exists any criminal threat to Canadian security.

10:3 THE FEES

There are fees associated with the various applications for coming to Canada. See Schedule 4 (page 228) for the relevant fees at the time of the preparation of these materials.

Apart from the two types of fees discussed in more detail below, you have to consider the fees related to medical examination(s), police certificates and language tests. There may be additional fees, like for example the fee required by the individual provinces in the case of an application under a Provincial Nominee Program.

10:3.1 Application fee

This fee must be paid for the principal applicant and any accompanying family member at the time of the application. This fee is not refundable.

10:3.2 Right of permanent residence fee

This fee is to be paid in the case of applications for permanent residence in Canada. It is to be paid for the principal applicant and accompanying spouse or common-law partner after the application is made and before CIC can issue you your permanent residence visa.

This fee is refundable if:

◆ you cancel your application;

◆ CIC does not issue a visa to you;

◆ you end up not using your visa.

10:4 WHAT HAPPENS AFTER YOU MAKE AN APPLICATION

In general, visa offices have their own processes and time frames for processing applications. However, after you submit your application each visa office will do the following.

◆ Ensure that your application is complete (i.e. that you have included the required fees, information and supporting documents). If your application is not complete, the package will be returned to you.

◆ Begin processing your application if the application is complete. You will receive a letter confirming that your application has been received and is being processed and giving you the number of your file, some basic instructions for contact with the visa office and an outline as to future processing steps.

During the decision-making process, the office may contact you if further documentation is required and if a personal interview is required.

10:5 THE INTERVIEW

The decision of whether or not you will be called for an interview before you are issued a visa for coming to Canada rests with the immigration officer processing your file. Your spouse or common-law partner and dependent children age 18 or over may also be asked to come to the interview.

At the interview, you may be questioned about your job, experience, education, reasons for migrating, plans and preparations, family, health, financial situation or past difficulties with the law. If you are making an application for permanent residence, there may also be questions to determine your ability to settle successfully in Canada. In the case of a temporary residence application, the immigration officer will have to be satisfied, among other things, that you intend to leave Canada at the end of your authorised stay.

It is important to make sure that, prior to the interview, you review the materials and forms that were included in your application. The questions you will be asked at the interview will often be largely clarification or verification of information on the forms. In terms of the documents that you should bring with you to the interview, check with the visa office beforehand and make sure that you obtain a list. You should make sure that you have with you the originals of the documents, the copies of which you included in the application.

Last, it would be to your advantage if you:

◆ make it to the interview on time;

◆ are polite and courteous to the people you interact with at the visa office;

◆ dress professionally;

◆ organise the documents you have with you as well as possible, so that if asked for an item, you can provide it without difficulty.

It is also a good idea to make a note, to the best of your ability, of what was asked and answered at the interview and keep it. It may be useful to have it at a later time.

10:6 THE DECISION WITH REGARD TO YOUR APPLICATION

10:6.1 Applications for permanent residence

If your application is successful, you will be asked to submit your passports to the visa office where you applied. You will receive permanent visas for Canada. Please note that the validity of your visa cannot exceed the validity of your passport. The Canadian visa office may request that your passport be renewed prior to submission.

The validity date of your permanent resident visa is based on the earlier of:

◆ your passport validity dates or your family's members passport validity dates; or

- the medical validity dates; medical examination results are valid for 12 months after the initial medical examination.

You will also be issued a Confirmation of Permanent Residence (COPR) form that will contain all of your identification information, as well as a photo and your signature.

If your application is refused, you will be informed of that in writing.

10:6.2 Applications for temporary residence

If your application is refused, you will be informed in writing. If your application is approved, the following will happen.

- If you applied for a **work permit**, you will receive a letter confirming the approval; when you arrive in Canada, you must show this letter to an officer at the port of entry who will issue you the work permit.

- If you applied for a **study permit**, you will receive a letter of introduction confirming the approval. Please note that this letter is not your study permit; when you arrive in Canada, you will have to show this letter to the immigration officials who will issue you a study permit at that time.

You will also be issued a Temporary Resident Visa for coming to Canada.

10:7 THE APPEAL PROCESS

If your application for coming to Canada is refused, your documents will be returned to you with an explanation of why your application was refused. Any documents found to be fraudulent will not be returned to you.

In some circumstances, you have the right either to appeal or seek judicial review of the decision of the immigration officer to reject your application. This includes the case where you have applied for permanent resident status and your application was denied. If you wish to challenge a decision to reject your application, you should consult competent counsel.

11

Arriving in Canada

Once you have your visa for coming to Canada, it is time to get ready. Below are a few issues that you might find of interest.

11:1 AT THE PORT OF ENTRY

11:1.1 Arriving in Canada with a permanent residence visa

At the port of entry, you will be required to present the Confirmation of Permanent Residence (COPR) to an immigration officer, along with your visa. The officer will ensure the following.

♦ Your visa has not expired:
   please note that the expiry date is listed on your visa, and the visa cannot be used for entry into Canada after that date. It is important to remember that permanent residence visas cannot be extended, so it is essential that you use your visa for entry into Canada within the time allowed. **If you do not use your visa within its validity, you must reapply for immigration to Canada.**

◆ You and your accompanying family members have valid passports:

  you cannot obtain permanent residence with a diplomatic, government service or public affairs passport. You have to have with you a valid regular, private passport.

◆ You are of good character and are in good health:

  you will be asked questions like the ones you answered on your Application for Permanent Residence in Canada.

◆ You have proof of the funds required:

  you must also show proof of your funds at this time.

If there are no problems, the immigration officer will authorise your entry into Canada as a permanent resident. The officer will also use the information on your COPR to have your Permanent Residence Card[1] sent to you by registered mail.

11:1.2 Arriving in Canada for temporary residence

When you arrive in Canada, an officer from Citizenship and Immigration Canada (CIC) will ask you a few questions. You will not be allowed into Canada if you give false or incomplete information, or if you do not satisfy the officer that you are suitable for entry into Canada. You will also have to satisfy the officer that you will leave Canada at the end of the temporary period authorised for your stay.

---

[1]The Permanent Residence Card is a document which allows you to travel to Canada on commercial carriers and in many cases will be seen as de facto proof of residency in Canada.

If you are coming as a temporary foreign worker, you should ensure that you have with you copies, preferably the originals, of supporting documents such as employment letters and proof of educational credentials.

All of the above apply both to those who must obtain Temporary Resident Visas in order to come to Canada, and to those exempted from this procedure.[2]

If all goes well, you will be admitted into Canada and advised as to how long you may stay in the country. You may be asked to make a cash deposit for security if the officer believes you need extra motivation to respect the conditions of your temporary stay in Canada. The deposit will be returned after you leave Canada if you have not breached the conditions imposed on you.

Children under the age of 16 should bring identification showing who they are. Bring a letter from the parent of a minor child you are travelling with, if you are not the child's parent or guardian. If you are coming with your child and are the only guardian, bring documentation showing the child has no other guardians, for example: a court order to that effect.

You may not work in Canada or go to school without permission.[3] You will be asked to leave Canada if you work or study without permission (often via a removal order).

[2]See Schedules 2 and 3 (pages 225 and 227).
[3]For information about exceptions to these rules, see Chapters 7 and 8.

Officers from CIC will have to take enforcement action against any person who does not respect the conditions of their visit to Canada.

Once in Canada, if you wish to change the conditions of your visit or stay in Canada, you can apply to do so, as mentioned in Chapters 7, 8 and 9. Your application may be approved; however, make sure that you apply at least a month before your status as a temporary resident expires.

11:2 CUSTOMS ISSUES/RESTRICTIONS ON WHAT YOU CAN BRING INTO CANADA

11:2.1 Plant and animal products, live animals

Plant and animal products brought with you into Canada must be declared at the port of entry. Please be advised that there are monetary penalties for not declaring such items.

Meat and dairy products, nuts, plants, fruits and live animals, if allowed into Canada, may require permits issued in Canada in advance, and/or certificates from the country of origin. Without the required documents, entry is not permitted. Some products, plants or animals may be seized and disposed of, or ordered removed from Canada. Others may require treatment before they can stay. The costs related to disposal, quarantine or treatment of such items are the responsibility of the traveller.

For more details about this topic, visit the site of the Canadian Food Inspection Agency (CFIA) at **www.inspection.gc.ca/english/corpaffr/publications/ declare.shtml**.

You can also contact CFIA at **www.inspection.gc.ca** Tel: 1-800-442-2342.

Depending on what you intend to bring into Canada, you may have to request additional information from the individual provinces and other federal departments/agencies such as Environment Canada and the Canada Customs and Revenue Agency.

11:2.2 Cash

You should be aware that Canadian legislation requires persons entering Canada to declare cash funds of CDN$10,000 or more. You will have to disclose these funds to a Canadian official upon arrival. Cash funds means money, securities in bearer form (stocks, bonds, debentures, treasury bills, etc) and negotiable instruments in bearer form (bank drafts, travellers' cheques, money orders, etc). Failure to disclose can result in fines and imprisonment.

11:2.3 Other items that may have to be declared

At the port of entry, if you are not sure whether an item should be declared or not, it is best to err on the side of declaring it.

All weapons must be declared. Guns can be brought into Canada only under certain circumstances. Weapons such as mace and pepper spray cannot be brought into Canada under any circumstances. As for alcohol and tobacco products, there are limits on the quantities that you can bring into Canada with you. For more information on this topic, please visit the site of Canada Customs and Revenue Agency at **www.ccra-adrc.gc.ca**.

12

Immigrating to Quebec

If you wish to live, work or study in Quebec, you should be aware that there are additional steps to the application processes discussed in Chapters 3, 4 and 6 to 8. This chapter, while not covering the procedure for temporary and permanent immigration to Quebec in detail, will provide you with some relevant information and a roadmap that should help you find your way on your own. For more information, you can always refer to the following web site: **www.immigration-quebec.gouv.qc.ca/anglais**.

12:1 COMING TO QUEBEC AS A SKILLED WORKER/PERMANENT WORKER

There are three immigration programmes for skilled workers in Quebec, each with its own set of eligibility requirements.

The **Assured Employment Program** allows a skilled worker who has received a job offer from a Quebec employer to immigrate to the province, provided that the following conditions are met.

◆ The employer has been in business in Quebec for over 12 months.

◆ The employer undertakes in writing to reserve the job for the particular foreign worker.

◆ The employer demonstrates that s/he made reasonable efforts to hire a qualified Quebec resident but was unable to fill the position locally; this is not a requirement if the position sought to be filled is one of: electrical and electronics engineers, computer engineers (except software engineers), computer systems analysts and consultants, software engineers, mechanical engineering technologists and technicians, machinists and machining and tooling inspectors – setter-operator for computer controlled machine tools.

◆ The employer is sure that local manpower cannot be trained to fill this position within not more than one year.

◆ The employer offers a position that complies with legal and regulatory obligations.

◆ The worker can show, at the time of selection, that s/he satisfies the conditions of the position offered and the conditions governing access to the occupation as defined in the National Occupational Classification (NOC)[1].

◆ The worker possesses, if required, certification of eligibility or a work permit from a professional body or association.

◆ The worker undertakes in writing to occupy this position as soon as he enters Canada.

[1]See Chapter 2 for more information about the NOC.

In the case of the **Occupations in Demand Program**, the applicant, to be admitted, must satisfy the following requirements:

◆ practise in one of the occupations in demand at the time the application is made;[2]

◆ has at least six months of work experience in the particular occupation; and

◆ upon arrival in Quebec, has the required funds available to support himself/herself and, if applicable, the accompanying family members for three months.

A single individual must have at his/her disposal at least CDN$2,300 to meet basic needs during the first three months in Quebec. Approximately CDN$1,000 must be added to this sum for each member of the family accompanying him/her (spouse, common-law spouse and children).

Under the **Employability and Occupational Mobility Program**, the following main factors are considered: training,[3] work experience, age, knowledge of French and English, previous visits or ties with Quebec, at least six months of work experience and the minimum funds required mentioned in the category above.

Under the second and third of the three programmes you have the option of submitting and having assessed, free of charge, a Preliminary Application for Immigration form. If

---

[2]See **www.immigration-quebec.gouv.qc.ca/anglais** for a list of occupations in demand at the time of making your application.
[3]For a list of favoured training list, see
www.immigration-quebec.gouv.qc.ca/anglais.

you are found to qualify at this initial stage, you will be sent within three months the additional forms to apply.

As part of the process, you will apply for a Certificat de sélection du Québec (CSQ). If you suceed in obtaining it, you can then apply for immigration visas to the relevant visa office.

12:2 COMING TO QUEBEC AS A SPONSORED FAMILY MEMBER

In the case of sponsoring family members and relatives, if the sponsorship application is accepted, in accordance with the usual process, the sponsoree's permanent residence application will be sent to the relevant visa office. In addition, the province of Quebec will also be advised of the fact that the sponsor has met the federal sponsorship requirements. The Ministere de Relations avec les citoyens et de l'Immigration (MRCI) will mail and request that additional forms be completed, both by the sponsor and by the person(s) to be sponsored, such as the Application for Selection Certificate and the undertaking form (Formulaire d'engagement). Provided that the sponsor meets Quebec's eligibility criteria,[4] the sponsorship undertaking will be accepted and the relevant visa office will be informed of that as well. A Quebec Selection Certificate (CSQ) may be issued to the sponsoree and, at that point, the processing of the permanent residence application will begin at the relevant visa office.

---

[4]The Quebec eligibility criteria are similar to the federal ones; for more details, including an updated income scale visit
www.immigration-quebec.gouv.qc.ca/anglais.

12:3 COMING TO QUEBEC AS A BUSINESS IMMIGRANT

Quebec has three categories of business immigration: the Entrepreneur, Investor and Self-Employed Programs. The eligibility criteria are as follows:

For the **Entrepreneur Program**, you must:

◆ have, along with your accompanying married or common-law spouse, where applicable, lawfully acquired net assets of at least CDN$300,000;

◆ have at least three years of management experience (planning, supervision and control of human, physical and financial resources) acquired in a lawful and profitable business (agricultural, industrial or commercial);

◆ submit a business plan to establish or acquire a business in Quebec that you will manage yourself or as a partner in management and day-to-day operations, and that will employ at least three Quebec residents other than yourself and members of your immediate family;

◆ satisfy the following conditions for at least one year in the three years after you become a permanent resident:
a) you must control at least $33^1/3\%$ of the capital of an eligible Canadian business:
b) you must manage the corporation actively and continuously;
c) you must create the equivalent of at least one full-time equivalent job for Canadian citizens or permanent residents other than yourself and members of your family.

For the **Investor Program**, you must:

◆ have a minimum net worth of CDN$800,000 acquired through lawful economic activities;

◆ have at least three years of management experience (planning, supervision and control of human, material and financial resources) in a profitable and lawful business (agricultural, industrial or commercial), in government or with an international agency;

◆ undertake to invest a minimum of CDN$400,000, for five years, by signing an agreement with a financial intermediary.[5]

For the **Self-Employed Worker Program**, you must:

◆ come to Quebec to create your own job by practicing an occupation in your own account;

◆ possess a lawfully acquired minimum net worth of CDN$100,000 along with your accompanying married or common-law spouse, where applicable;

◆ have at least two years of experience as a self-employed worker in the occupation you plan to pursue in Quebec.

If you meet the eligibility requirements under any of the three categories mentioned above and you wish to learn more about the application process, visit **www.immigration-quebec.gouv.qc.ca/anglais**.

[5]For contact information relating to financial intermediaries, visit **www.immigration-quebec.gouv.qc.ca/anglais**.

12:4 COMING TO QUEBEC AS A TEMPORARY WORKER

If a Quebec employer wishes to hire you, they will have to make an application to Quebec's version of the Human Resources Development Canada (as discussed in Chapter 7, section 7:1.2) known as MRCI.

The application to MRCI will include additional fees and the completed form for the Certificate of Acceptance to Quebec. The factors that MRCI will take into consideration in assessing the employer's application are similar to those discussed in Chapter 7, section 7:1.2a. HRSDC and MRCI will issue a joint decision on the basis of which you will be able to apply for a work permit as discussed in Chapter 7.

Please note that specific procedures apply to the hiring of temporary foreign workers in the following occupations:

◆ film industry workers;

◆ information technology industry workers;

◆ optics-phonotics industry workers;

◆ health care workers – nurses, doctors, clinical instructors;

◆ holders of a research chair;

◆ seasonal agricultural workers;

◆ live-in caregivers.

For more information about the special procedure, visit **www.immigration-quebec.gouv.qc.ca/anglais**.

12:5 STUDYING IN QUEBEC

If you have applied to an educational institution in Quebec, in order to obtain a study permit you will require a Quebec Certificate of Acceptance (CAQ) or Certificat d'acceptation du Québec. The educational institution will let you know how to apply for one. However, you will not have to obtain a CAQ if:

◆ you have obtained a scholarship from the Canadian International Development Agency (CIDA) or under the Programme canadien de bourses de la Francophonie, provided that the scholarship covers all of your expenses; otherwise the CAQ for study purposes is required. However, your spouse and children must obtain a CAQ in order to study in Quebec;

◆ you are planning to study for six months or less;

◆ you are participating in a Canadian government assistance programme for developing countries.

The CAQ will be valid for three years. If you have not completed your studies in Quebec by the end of those three years, you will have to apply for a CAQ again.

Appendix
Sample of Visa Office
Specific Instructions

Citizenship and
Immigration Canada

Citoyenneté et
Immigration Canada

IMMIGRATION

Canada

Application for Permanent Residence

Visa Office Specific Instructions

London

Table of Contents

This is not a legal document. For legal information, please refer to the *Immigration and Refugee Protection Act*, 2001 and *Immigration Regulations*, 2002.

Aussi disponible en français

IMM 7023 E (06-2002)

Canada

209

Appendix A
Checklist

Gather documents as listed. Check (☑) each item on the checklist and attach it to your documents (a paper clip will do). Place all documents in a sealed envelope. **Do not send originals**. Send notarized photocopies of all documents **except** the the police certificates, which must be **originals**. If your documents are not in English or French, send a notarized (certified) translation with a photocopy of the originals.

1 **FORMS**	
See the **"Filling Out the Forms"** section on our Web site at www.cic.gc.ca/skilled for specific instructions on how to complete the questions on each of the following forms.	
APPLICATION FOR PERMANENT RESIDENCE IN CANADA Check that it is complete and signed and that you have included (not stapled) four specified photographs (with names on the back for each applicant) for each member of your family and yourself. (See box 15 of this checklist for further information on photo specifications.)	☐
SCHEDULE 1: BACKGROUND DECLARATION Include a Schedule 1 form completed by: • the principal applicant • spouse or common-law partner • each dependent child over 18 years of age	☐
SCHEDULE 3: ECONOMIC CLASSES – FEDERAL SKILLED WORKERS Completed by the principal applicant.	☐
ADDITIONAL FAMILY INFORMATION Completed by: • the principal applicant • spouse or common-law partner • each dependent child over the age of 18 years	☐
AUTHORITY TO RELEASE INFORMATION TO DESIGNATED INDIVIDUALS Include this form only if you wish us to release information regarding your application to someone other than yourself. Be advised that, if and for as long as you have designated an agent to represent you, we will communicate only with that person or firm. Any processing enquiries you may have must be made through that agent. Any such enquiries that you send directly to this office will neither be answered nor acknowledged.	☐
2 **IDENTITY AND CIVIL STATUS DOCUMENTS** • Birth, marriage, final divorce, annulment or separation certificates for you and spouse • Death certificate for former spouse if applicable • Photocopy of **citizenship certificate** or **permanent resident visa** (formerly called "immigrant visa") for any family members who are Canadian citizens or permanent residents of Canada	☐

3   CHILDREN'S INFORMATION (if applicable)
- Children's birth certificates (which name their parents)
- Adoption papers for adopted dependent children
- Proof of custody for children under the age of 18 and proof that the children may be removed from the jurisdiction of the court
- If the children will not accompany you to Canada, proof that you have fulfilled any obligation stated in custody agreements
- Proof of **continuous full-time studies** of all dependent children aged 22 or over, including:
  - complete school records/transcripts since attaining age 22
  - letters from the schools indicating the number of hours of classes attended per day, and the number of days attended per week
  - proof of full financial support by parents since reaching age 22

4   TRAVEL DOCUMENTS AND PASSPORTS
- Passports or travel documents for you, your spouse or common-law partner and your dependent children. Include only copies of pages showing the passport number, date of issue and expiry, your photo, name, date and place of birth.
- If you live in a country different from your nationality include a photocopy of your visa for the country where you currently live. Note that all prospective immigrants must hold a valid regular passport; diplomatic, official, service or public affairs passports are not valid for immigration to Canada.

5   PROOF OF RELATIONSHIP IN CANADA (if applicable)
Proof of relationship to your close relative in Canada, such as birth, marriage or adoption certificates and proof of that person's status in Canada: photocopy of the *Record of Landing* (IMM 1000) or proof of Canadian citizenship such as a photocopy of pages of a Canadian passport or Canadian citizenship card.

6   EDUCATION/TRAINING/QUALIFICATIONS
For you and your spouse or common-law partner:
- **Post-secondary education documents:** vocational or technical certificates or diplomas;
- **College or university documents:** certification of completion and the graduation degree, diploma, or certificate issued by the college or university and the evaluation committee;
- **Transcripts:** original transcripts of all degrees must be submitted in university-sealed envelopes.
- **Professional qualifications certificates:** notarized professional qualification certificates should be submitted if available. (e.g.. Engineer, Computer Programmer, Accountant, Economist, Translator/Interpreter, Architect etc.)

7   WORK EXPERIENCE
For you and your spouse or common-law partner:
- notarized employment contracts from your present and past employers, accompanied by an English or French translation
- Original and up-to-date letters of reference from your past and current employers. Letters must be written on company letterhead and show the company's full address, telephone and fax numbers, and be stamped with the company's official seal.

Letters must include all of the following information:
- the specific period of your employment with the company
- the positions you have held during the period of employment and the time spent in each position
- your main responsibilities in each position
- your total annual salary plus benefits
- the signature of your immediate supervisor or the personnel officer of the company
- a business card of the person signing

If you cannot provide a reference from your current employer, provide a written explanation.

8	**WORK EXPERIENCE**

8 WORK EXPERIENCE ☐

For you and your spouse or common-law partner:
- notarized employment contracts from your present and past employers, accompanied by an English or French translation
- Original and up-to-date letters of reference from your past and current employers. Letters must be written on company letterhead and show the company's full address, telephone and fax numbers, and be stamped with the company's official seal.

Letters must include all of the following information:
- the specific period of your employment with the company
- the positions you have held during the period of employment and the time spent in each position
- your main responsibilities in each position
- your total annual salary plus benefits
- the signature of your immediate supervisor or the personnel officer of the company
- a business card of the person signing

If you cannot provide a reference from your current employer, provide a written explanation.

9 ARRANGED EMPLOYMENT (if applicable) ☐
If you are currently working in Canada under a work permit, provide a photocopy of the permit.

10 PROOF OF LANGUAGE PROFICIENCY ☐
Refer to instructions in the "**Language Assessment Information**" section of our Web site. If you are claiming proficiency at any level in English and/or French, submit one of the following:

- **Test results from an approved language-testing organization:** We strongly recommend that you submit test results if you are claiming proficiency in a language that is not your native language. If you choose to send the reports to us directly, you must provide the **original**. Photocopies are unacceptable. Language test results must not be older than one year upon submission.

or

- **Other evidence in writing:**
  - Your written submission detailing your training in, and use of, English and/or French;
  - Official documentation of education in English or French;
  - Official documentation of work experience in English or French.
  - Other applicable documentation.

11 NON-ACCOMPANYING FAMILY MEMBERS DECLARATION (if applicable): ☐
If you have a spouse, common-law partner or dependent children and you do not intend to include them in your application for permanent residence, submit with your application a notarized statutory declaration stating your intention to proceed to Canada without your family members, and confirming that you understand that your family members must meet immigration requirements in their own right if they wish to join you in Canada.

12 SETTLEMENT FUNDS ☐
(Refer to the "**Proof of Funds**" section of our Web site (www.cic.gc.ca/skilled) or the *Guide for Federal Skilled Worker Applicants* for exact figures and instructions.)
Provide proof of unencumbered and readily transferable funds in a convertible currency available for settlement in Canada (for you and your family members):
- current bank certification letter; or
- evidence of savings balance; or
- fixed or time deposit statements.

13 POLICE CERTIFICATES AND CLEARANCES ☐
- **Original** police certificates of good conduct or clearances, from each country/state/territory in which you and everyone in your family aged 18 years or over have lived for six months or longer since reaching the age of 18.
- Submit original fingerprints directly to the authorities conducting the police checks
- If you have obtained police certificates from countries where the authorities will forward results directly to us, attach a brief explanatory note to your application.

14	**FEE PAYMENT**	☐
	Consult the **Fees** section of our Web site or the *Guide for Skilled Worker Applicants* to calculate your fees. Use a bank draft to pay the full immigration processing fees in Canadian dollars. **Do not enclose cash**.	
15	**PHOTO REQUIREMENTS**	☐
	Supply the number of photographs requested under "**Application for Permanent Residence in Canada**" in box 1 of the *Checklist* and follow the instructions provided in Appendix C: Photo Specifications.	

Once you have assembled all the required documents, send them to:

Immigration and Medical Division
Canadian High Commission
38 Grosvenor Street
London, UK
W1X 0AA

Appendix B
Obtaining Police Certificates/Clearances

Everyone in your family aged 18 years or older requires a police certificate from each country they have lived in for six months or longer. You must provide **original** police certificates to indicate whether you or your family members have any criminal record. We will also conduct our own checks.

It is your responsibility to contact the relevant authorities to obtain the necessary police certificates or clearances. In some countries you will have to apply to municipal, provincial, federal or similar governmental agencies for your record.

The authority responsible for issuing your police certificate or clearance may require a processing fee and additional documentation such as photographs, fingerprints or details of your addresses and periods of residence in that country. Some require a letter from Canadian immigration authorities confirming that you have applied to immigrate to Canada and that you must obtain evidence of any criminal record as part of the processing of your application. The enclosed letter, titled **Request For Police Certificates/Clearances,** is provided for this purpose. It identifies your file reference number from Canada Immigration by the number commencing with M992000 followed by your surname. Please make photocopies if you require additional copies.

If you have a conviction in Canada, you must seek a pardon from the National Parole Board of Canada before you apply for immigration to Canada. The address is:

Clemency and Pardons Division
National Parole Board
410 Laurier Avenue West
Ottawa, ON, Canada
K1A 0R1
Fax: 1-613-941-4981
Web site: www.npb-cnlc.gc.ca (application forms can be downloaded from the site)

The examples listed below may help you to understand what is required.

1. Sunil, an Indian citizen, is living in the UK. Sunil has also been living in India and Dubai. He must obtain police clearances from all these countries.

    Sunil contacts the Indian High Commission in London and the police authorities in The United Arab Emirates for information on how to obtain police certificates covering the periods he resided in India and Dubai. He then writes to the relevant offices and obtains his police clearance certificates by mail.

    For the UK, Sunil contacts the local police who advise him that under the UK Data Protection Act, he can obtain information to confirm whether or not he had any convictions. A resident of London, Sunil writes to:

    Metropolitan Police
    Subject Access Office
    10 Broadway
    London SW1H 0BG

    He also learns that local police keep application forms with details on how to apply and pay the processing fee. If Sunil had lived outside London, he would have applied to the regional police authority for the district where he resided.

2. Flora had been working in Canada for the past two years on a temporary work visa. Flora has also been living in Sweden and Saudi Arabia. She must obtain police clearances from all these countries.

For Canada, Flora writes to:

Royal Canadian Mounted Police
NCO I/C Civil Section
Identification Services
PO Box 8885
Ottawa, Ontario K1G 3M8
Canada

With this letter she encloses the **Request for Police Certificates/Clearances** which she has completed with her personal details and a full set of fingerprints, taken and certified by the police (fingerprints taken by private or commercial agencies are not acceptable).

Flora contacts the Swedish Embassy for information on obtaining a police certificate for her period of residence in Sweden.

Finally, Flora contacts the Saudi Arabian Embassy and discovers that Saudi Arabia does not issue police certificates. Therefore, she encloses a covering letter in her immigration application, explaining that she was unable to obtain a Saudi police certificate with the written advice from the Saudi authorities stating that police certificates are not issued.

Immigration Canada is aware that a small number of countries, including Saudi Arabia, do not readily issue police certificates or a similar document.

3. Gerard Foley is completing the third year of his PhD in the USA. Prior to this he lived in Ireland. He must obtain police clearances from both of these countries.

For the USA, Gerard writes to:

U.S. Department of Justice
The Federal Bureau of Investigation
CJIS Division – for attention of Special Correspondence Unit
1000 Custer Hollow Road
Clarksburg, West Virginia 26306
USA

He encloses a certified cheque or money order for US$18.00, payable to the US Treasury Department, and a full set of fingerprints, taken and certified by his local police (fingerprints taken by private or commercial agencies are not acceptable), with full name, date and place of birth included on his fingerprint form.

Gerard contacts the Garda police authorities in Ireland, who are able to provide him with a clearance certificate.

Canadian High Commission   **Haut Commissariat du Canada**

<table>
<tr><td>

Immigration and Medical Division
Canadian High Commission
Macdonald House
38 Grosvenor Street
London W1X 0AA
Fax: (0171) 258 6506

</td><td>

Service d'immigration
Canadian High Commission
Macdonald House
38 Grosvenor Street
London W1X 0AA
Fax: (0171) 258 6506

</td></tr>
</table>

Request For Police Certificates/Clearances

FILE NUMBER: M99-2000	SURNAME:

To Police or Relevant Authorities:

The person who has completed the authorization form below is applying for admission to Canada as a permanent resident. To meet Canadian immigration requirements, each member of his/her family aged 18 years and over requires an original Police Certificate/Clearance of no criminal conviction.

We would ask that the Certificates be provided to the bearer of this letter, who will then forward them to the High Commission. If this is not possible, the Certificates should be sent directly to the High Commission, quoting the above File Number.

Thank you for your cooperation.

The High Commission

Authorization by Visa Applicant for Release of Police and Court Records
To be completed by applicant:

I hereby authorize the Police or Relevant Authorities in _____ (name country) to disclose any details of previous criminal convictions to the Canadian High Commission, London, England, for visa purposes only.

Surname:
Given Names:
Maiden or other Surname(s) Used:
Name in Original Script (i.e. Arabic, Chinese etc.):
Date & Place of Birth:
Nationality:
Sex:

All Addresses while Resident in _____ **(name country)**

Dates (from - to)		Home address
/ / /	/ / /	
/ / /	/ / /	
/ / /	/ / /	

Signature Of Applicant: _____ Date: _____

Appendix C
Photo Specifications

Notes to the applicant

TAKE THIS WITH YOU TO THE PHOTOGRAPHER

- Immigration photographs are **not** the same as passport photographs.
- Make sure that you provide the correct number of photographs specified in the *Checklist*.

Notes to the photographer

The photographs must:

- show a full front view of the person's head and shoulders showing full face centred in the middle of the photograph;
- have a **plain white background**;
- be identical (black and white or colour) produced from the same untouched negative, or exposed simultaneously by a split-image or multi-lens camera;

The photographs must:

- measure between 25 mm and 35 mm (1" and 1 3/8") from chin to crown
- have a 35 mm x 45 mm (1 3/8" x 1 3/4") finished size

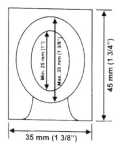

Appendix D
Medical Instructions

Everyone included in your application, whether accompanying you to Canada or not, is required to undergo a medical examination with a physician on our list of designated doctors.

Do not initiate any medical tests until you receive the medical form and instructions.

Instructions for the medical will be mailed to you after your application has been assessed and a positive selection decision is made. You will receive a medical form for you (and your dependants if applicable), instructions for arranging medical examinations, and a list of doctors in your area who are authorized to conduct medical examinations. You must make an appointment with the designated doctor of your choice in your area. Proper identification (passport or birth certificate) for each family member must be presented to the medical practitioner.

The applicant should contact the doctor as soon as possible. All fees pertaining to the examination and mailing, as well as any tests or examinations we may require, are the responsibility of the applicant

Medical reports and X-rays arising from the immigration medical examination become the property of the Canadian Immigration medical authorities and will not be returned to the applicant.

The permanent residence visa has the same validity as the medical results, that is, 12 months from the date of the first medical examination.

> **Note:** If you are a divorced or separated parent, a minor child of whom you have joint or sole custody is considered your dependent child, even if he or she usually lives with the other parent and is not accompanying you to Canada.

Schedules

SCHEDULE 1
VISA POSTS

Where to Apply for a Permanent Resident Visa

If you have been lawfully admitted for at least one year to one of the following countries, provinces or territories (or are a citizen of);	You must apply at the Canadian Visa Office corresponding to the country in this column:
Afghanistan	Islamabad
Albania	Rome
Algeria	Paris
Andorra	Paris
Angola	Pretoria
Anguilla	Port of Spain
Anhui	Beijing
Antigua & Barbuda	Port of Spain
Argentina	Buenos Aires
Armenia	Moscow
Aruba	Caracas
Ascension	Accra
Ashmore and Cartier Island	Sydney
Australia	Sydney
Austria	Vienna
Azerbaijan	Ankara
Bahamas	Kingston
Bahrain	London
Bangladesh	Singapore
Barbados	Port of Spain
Belarus	Warsaw
Belau, Republic of (or Palau)	Manila
Belgium	Paris
Belize	Guatemala City
Benin	Accra

Bermuda	Buffalo
Bhutan	New Delhi
Bolivia	Lima
Bonaire	Caracas
Bora Bora	Sydney
Boznia-Herzegovina	Vienna
Botswana	Pretoria
Brazil	Sao Paulo
British Indian Ocean Territory	Colombo
Brunei	Singapore
Bulgaria	Bucharest
Burkina-Faso	Abidjan
Burma (Myanmar, Union of)	Singapore
Burundi	Nairobi
Cambodia	Singapore
Cameroon`	Abidjan
Canada (for temporary lawful resident only)	Buffalo, or office responsible for your country of citizenship or, if stateless, your country of habitual residence (see this list).
Canary Islands	Paris
Cape Verde	Abidjan
Caroline Islands	Manila
Cayman Islands	Kingston
Central African Republic	Abidjan
Chad	Abidjan
Channel Islands	London
Chile	Santiago
China (see People's Republic of China)	
Cnoiseul	Sydney
Christmas Island	Sydney
Cocos (Keeling) Island	Sydney
Colombia	Bogota
Comoros Island	Nairobi
Cook Island	Sydney
Costa Rica	Guatemala City
Croatia	Vienna
Cuba	Havana
Curaçao	Caracas
Cyprus	Damascus
Czech Republic	Vienna
Democratic Republic of the Congo 7/15/2003	Abidjan
Denmark	London
Djibouti	Nairobi
Dominica	Port of Spain
Dominican Republic	Port-au-Prince
East Timor	Singapore
Easter Island	Chile
Ecuador	Bogota
Egypt	Cairo
El Salvador	Guatemala City

England	London
Equatorial Guinea	Abidjan
Eritrea	Nairobi
Estonia	Warsaw
Ethiopia	Nairobi
Falkland Islands	Buenos Aires
Faroe Islands	London
Federal Republic of Yugoslavia	Vienna
Fiji	Sydney
Finland	London
France	Paris
French Guiana	Port-au-Prince
French Polynesia	Sydney
Fujian (PRC's province)	Hong Kong
Gabon	Abidjan
Gambia	Accra
Gambier Island	Sydney
Gaza Strip (Palestinian Authority)	Tel Aviv
Georgia	Ankara
Germany	Berlin
Ghana	Accra
Gibraltar	Paris
Greece	Rome
Greenland	London
Grenada	Port of Spain
Guadalcanal	Sydney
Guadeloupe	Port-au-Prince
Guam	Manila
Guangdong (PRC's province)	Hong Kong
Guangxi (PRC's province)	Hong Kong
Guatemala	Guatemala City
Guinea (Refugees apply in Accra)	Abidjan
Guinea-Bissau	Abidjan
Guyana	Port of Spain
Hainan (PRC's province)	Hong Kong
Haiti	Port-au-Prince
Honduras	Guatemala City
Hong Kong	Hong Kong
Huahine	Sydney
Hungary	Vienna
Iceland	London
India	New Delhi
Indonesia	Singapore
Iran	Damascus
Iraq	Damascus
Ireland	London
Isle of Man	London
Israel	Tel Aviv
Italy	Rome
Ivory Coast	Abidjan
Jamaica	Kingston
Japan	Manila
Jiangsu (PRC's province)	Beijing

Johnston Atoll	Manila
Jordan	Damascus
Kazakhstan	Moscow
Kenya	Nairobi
Kiribati	Sydney
Kosovo	Vienna
Kosrae (Micronesia)	Manila
Kuwait	London
Kyrgyzstan	Moscow
Laos	Singapore
Latvia	Warsaw
Lebanon	Damascus
Lesotho	Pretoria
Liberia	Accra
Libya	Paris
Liechtenstein	Paris
Lithuania	Warsaw
Lord Howe Island	Sydney
Loyalty Island	Sydney
Luxembourg	Paris
Macao	Hong Kong
Macedonia (Former Yugoslav Republic of)	Vienna
Madagascar (Republic of)	Nairobi
Maïo	Sydney
Malawi	Pretoria
Malaysia	Singapore
Maldives	Colombo
Mali	Abidjan
Malta	Rome
Marianas	Manila
Marie-Galante	Port-au-Prince
Marquesas Island	Sydney
Marshall Island	Manila
Martinique	Port-au-Prince
Maupiti	Sydney
Mauritania	Abidjan
Mauritius	Nairobi
Mexico	Mexico City
Micronesia (Federated States of)	Manila
Midway Island	Manila
Moldova	Bucharest
Monaco	Paris
Mongolia	Beijing
Montenegro	Vienna
Montserrat	Port of Spain
Moorea	Sydney
Morocco	Paris
Mozambique	Pretoria
Myanmar, Union of (Burma)	Singapore
Namibia	Pretoria
Nauru	Sydney
Nepal	New Delhi

Netherlands	Berlin
Nevis	Port of Spain
New Caledonia	Sydney
New Georgia	Sydney
New Ireland	Sydney
New Zealand	Sydney
Nicaragua	Guatemala City
Niger	Abidjan
Nigeria	Accra
Nine Island	Sydney
Norfolk Island	Sydney
North Korea	Beijing
Northern Ireland	London
Northern Mariana Island	Manila
Norway	London
Oman	London
Pakistan	Islamabad
Palau (or Republic of Belau)	Manila
Palestinian Authority (West Bank & Gaza Strip)	Tel Aviv
Panama	Guatemala City
Papua New Guinea	Sydney
Paraguay	Buenos Aires
People's Republic of China*	Beijing
*Exception: office serving provinces of: Fujian, Guangdong, Guangxi and Hainan is **Hong Kong**	
Peru	Lima
Philippines	Manila
Pitcairn Island	Sydney
Pohnpei (Micronesia)	Manila
Poland	Warsaw
Portugal (Azores, Madeira)	Paris
Puerto Rico	Port of Spain
Qatar	London
Raiatea	Sydney
Republic of Congo	Abidjan
Republic of Madagascar	Nairobi
Reunion	Nairobi
Romania	Bucharest
Russia	Moscow
Rwanda	Nairobi
Saba	Port-au-Prince
Samoa (American & Western)	Sydney
San Marino	Rome
Santa Isabel	Sydney
Sao Tome and Principe	Accra
Saudi Arabia	London
Scotland	London
Senegal	Abidjan
Serbia	Vienna
Seychelles	Nairobi
Shanghai	Beijing

Sierra Leone	Accra
Singapore	Singapore
Slovakia	Vienna
Slovenia	Vienna
Society Archipelago	Sydney
Solomon Island	Sydney
Somalia	Nairobi
South Africa	Pretoria
South Korea	Seoul
Spain	Paris
Sri Lanka	Colombo
St Pierre et Miquelon	Buffalo
St Barthelemay	Port-au-Prince
St Eustatius	Port-au-Prince
St Kitts	Port of Spain
St Lucia	Port of Spain
St Maarten/St Martin	Port-au-Prince
St Vincent and the Grenadines	Port of Spain
St Helena	Accra
Sudan	Cairo
Suriname	Port of Spain
Svalbard	London
Swaziland	Pretoria
Sweden	London
Switzerland	Paris
Syria	Damascus
Tahaa	Sydney
Tahiti	Sydney
Taiwan	Taÿpei
Tajikistan	Moscow
Tanzania	Nairobi
Thailand	Singapore
Togo	Accra
Tokeleau Island	Sydney
Tonga	Sydney
Tortola	Port of Spain
Trinidad & Tobago	Port of Spain
Tristan da Cunha	Accra
Truk Island (Micronesia)	Manila
Tuamotu Archipelago	Sydney
Tunisia	Paris
Turkey	Ankara
Turkmenistan	Ankara
Turks & Caicos	Kingston
Tuvalu	Sydney
Uganda	Nairobi
Ukraine	Kyiv
United Arab Emirates	London
Uruguay	Beunos Aires
US Trust Territories of the Patific Islands	Manila
USA	Buffalo
Uzbekistan	Moscow

Vanuatu	Sydney
Vatican City	Rome
Venezuela	Caracas
Vietnam	Singapore
Virgin Islands (British & US)	Port of Spain
Wake Island	Manila
Wales	London
Wallis & Futuna	Sydney
West Bank (Palestinian Authority)	Tel Aviv
Western Sahara	Paris
Yap Island (Micronesia)	Manila
Yemen	London
Zambia	Pretoria
Zhejiang (PRC's province)	Beijing
Zimbabwe	Pretoria

SCHEDULE 2
LIST OF COUNTRIES AND TERRITORIES WHOSE CITIZENS REQUIRE VISAS IN ORDER TO ENTER CANADA AS VISITORS[1]

A
Afghanistan
Albania
Algeria
Angola
Argentina
Armenia
Azerbaijan

B
Bahrain
Bangladesh
Belarus
Belize
Benin
Bhutan
Bolivia
Bosnia-Herzegovina
Brazil
Bulgaria
Burkina Faso
Burundi

C
Cambodia
Cameroon
Cape Verde
Central African
   Rep.
Chad
Chile
China, People's
   Rep. of
Colombia
Comoros
Congo, Democratic
   Rep. of the
Congo, Rep. of the
Croatia
Cuba
Czech Rep.

D
Djibouti
Dominica

Dominican Rep.

E
East Timor
Ecuador
Egypt
El Salvador
Equatorial Guinea
Eritrea
Estonia
Ethiopia

F
Fiji

G
Gabon
Gambia
Georgia
Ghana
Grenada
Guatemala
Guinea

[1]Citizens of these countries need a temporary resident visa (TRV) to visit and transit Canada. For more information about obtaining a TRV, see Chapter 9. For an updated list, visit the site of CIC at **www.cic.gc.ca**.

Guinea-Bissau
Guyana

H
Haiti
Honduras
Hungary

I
India
Indonesia
Iran
Iraq
Israel (only Israeli
citizens holding
valid Israeli 'Travel
Document in lieu
of National
Passport')
Ivory Coast

J
Jamaica
Jordan

K
Kazakhstan
Kenya
Kiribati
Korea, North
Kuwait
Kyrgyzstan

L
Laos
Latvia
Lebanon
Lesotho
Liberia
Libya
Lithuania

M
Macao S.A.R.
Macedonia
Madagascar

Malawi
Malaysia
Maldives Islands
Mali
Marshall Islands
Mauritania
Mauritius
Micronesia, Fed.
 States
Moldova
Mongolia
Morocco
Mozambique
Myanmar (Burma)

N
Nauru
Nepal
Nicaragua
Niger
Nigeria

O
Oman

P
Pakistan
Palau
Palestinian
 Authority
Panama
Paraguay
Peru
Philippines
Poland

Q
Qatar

R
Romania
Russia
Rwanda

S
Sao Tomé e
 Principe

Saudi Arabia,
Kingdom of Senegal
Seychelles
Sierra Leone
Slovak Rep.
Somalia
South Africa
Sri Lanka
Sudan
Surinam
Syria

T
Taiwan
Tajikistan
Tanzania
Thailand
Togo
Tonga
Trinidad and
 Tobago
Tunisia
Turkey
Turkmenistan
Tuvalu

U
Uganda
Ukraine
United Arab
 Emirates
Uruguay
Uzbekistan

V
Vanuatu
Venezuela
Vietnam

Y
Yemen
Yugoslavia

Z
Zambia
Zimbabwe

SCHEDULE 3
LIST OF PERSONS WHO DO NOT REQUIRE TEMPORARY RESIDENT VISAS TO VISIT OR TRANSIT CANADA[1]

◆ Citizens of Andorra, Antigua and Barbuda, Australia, Austria, Bahamas, Barbados, Belgium, Botswana, Brunei, Costa Rica, Cyprus, Denmark, Finland, France, Germany, Greece, Iceland, Ireland, Israel (National Passport holders only), Italy, Japan, Liechtenstein, Luxembourg, Malta, Mexico, Monaco, Namibia, Netherlands, New Zealand, Norway, Papua New Guinea, Portugal, Republic of Korea, St Kitts and Nevis, St Lucia, St Vincent, San Marino, Singapore, Solomon Islands, Spain, Swaziland, Sweden, Slovenia, Switzerland, United States, and Western Samoa.

◆ Persons lawfully admitted to the United States for permanent residence who are in possession of their alien registration card (Green card) or can provide other evidence of permanent residence.

◆ British citizens and British overseas citizens who are readmissible to the United Kingdom.

◆ Citizens of British dependent territories who derive their citizenship through birth, descent, registration or naturalisation in one of the British dependent territories of Anguilla, Bermuda, British Virgin Islands, Cayman Islands, Falkland Islands, Gibraltar, Montserrat, Pitcairn, St Helena or the Turks and Caicos Islands.

---

[1]Please note that the persons covered by Schedule 2 must nevertheless satisfy the requirements mentioned in Chapter 9, section 9:1, in order to be admitted in Canada.

◆ Persons holding a valid and subsisting Special Administrative Region passport issued by the Government of the Hong Kong Special Administrative Region of the People's Republic of China.

◆ Persons holding passports or travel documents issued by the Holy See.

SCHEDULE 4
FEE SCHEDULE FOR CITIZENSHIP AND IMMIGRATION SERVICES

The fees listed below are payable by applicants for processing applications of various types and for certain citizenship and immigration procedures. In general, fees are payable at the time of application. Please note that all fees are subject to change without notice. You should check with the relevant visa office or, if you are in Canada, with the nearest CIC office to confirm the correct amount that is applicable to you.

Note: All amounts are in Canadian dollars.

1. Applications for visas and permits

Permanent Resident Visas

Family Class applicants

Sponsorship application (per application)	$75
Principal applicant	$475

Principal applicant, if less than 22 years of age and not
a spouse or common-law partner (including a dependent
child of the sponsor, a child to be adopted and an
orphaned brother, sister, niece, nephew or grandchild) $75

A family member of the principal applicant who is
22 years of age or older, or is less than 22 years of age
and is a spouse or common-law partner $550

A family member of the principal applicant who is less
than 22 years of age and is not a spouse or common-law
partner $150

Note: Fees assessed for principal applicants and family members
under the Family Class are payable, along with the sponsorship
fee, when the sponsor files the sponsorship application.

Investor, Entrepreneur or Self-Employed Persons Class applicants

Principal applicant $1,050

A family member of the principal applicant who is
22 years of age or older, or is less than 22 years of age
and is a spouse or common-law partner $550

A family member of the principal applicant who is less
than 22 years of age and is not a spouse or common-law
partner $150

Other classes of applicants

Principal applicant $550

A family member of the principal applicant who is
22 years of age or older, or is less than 22 years of age
and is a spouse or common-law partner $550

A family member of the principal applicant who is less
than 22 years of age and is not a spouse or common-law
partner $150

Temporary Resident Visas

Single entry to Canada $75

Multiple entry $150

Note: The total will not exceed $400 per family, provided that the
family members all apply at the same time and place

Work Permits

Work permit $150

Note: This fee is per person, but the total amount will not exceed $450 in the case of a group of three or more performing artists and their staff who apply at the same time and place

Study Permits

Study permit $125

2. Fees for applications to remain in Canada as a permanent resident

Spouse or Common-law Partner in Canada Class

Sponsorship application (per application)	$75
Principal applicant	$475
A family member of the principal applicant who is 22 years of age or older, or is less than 22 years of age and is a spouse or common-law partner	$550
A family member of the principal applicant who is less than 22 years of age and is not a spouse or common-law partner	$150

Note: Fees assessed under the Spouse or Common-law Partner in Canada Class are payable, along with the sponsorship fee, when the sponsor files the sponsorship application. Refunds will be issued only if the sponsor withdraws the sponsorship application before processing of the application has begun. The $75 sponsorship fee will not normally be refunded.

Other applicants

Principal applicant	$550
A family member of the principal applicant who is 22 years of age or older, or is less than 22 years of age and is a spouse or common-law partner	$550
A family member of the principal applicant who is less than 22 years of age and is not a spouse or common-law partner	$150

Permit Holders Class

Applicant $325

3. Right of permanent residence fee (RPRF)

For the acquisition of permanent resident status $975

This fee is payable by principal applicants (with some exceptions) and accompanying spouses and common-law partners. It must be paid before the immigrant visa is issued overseas or before the applicant becomes a permanent resident in Canada.

The following applicants are not required to pay this fee:
* dependent children of a principal applicant or sponsor, a child to be adopted, or an orphaned brother, sister, niece, nephew or grandchild.

4. Other applications and services

Extension of Authorisation to Remain in Canada as a Temporary Resident

Application processing fee $75

Restoration of Temporary Resident Status

Application processing fee $200

Permanent Resident Cards*

Application processing fee $50

Renewal or replacement of lost, damaged or stolen card $50

*Existing permanent residents can apply for the card starting 15 October 2002

Certification and replacement of an immigration document

Application processing fee $30

After-hours examination

For entry into Canada, outside of normal service hours (payable at time of examination) $100*

*For the first four hours of the examination; $30 for each additional hour or part thereof

Alternative means of examination

Application processing fee $30

Immigration statistical data

Application processing fee $100*

*For the first 10 minutes or less of access to the Department's database in order to respond to such a request; $30 for each additional minute or less of access

Determination of rehabilitation

Application processing fee, if inadmissible on the grounds of serious criminality	$1,000
Application processing fee, if inadmissible on the grounds of criminality	$200

SCHEDULE 5
EXCERPT FROM THE NATIONAL OCCUPATIONS (NOC) LIST[1]

The following occupations are listed in Skill Type 0, Skill Level A or B of the NOC List.

A

0632	Accommodation Service Managers
5135	Actors and Comedians
1221	Administrative Officers
0114	Administrative Services Managers (other)
0312	Administrators – Post-Secondary Education and Vocational
2146	Aerospace Engineers
2222	Agricultural and Fish Products Inspectors
8252	Agricultural and Related Service Contractors and Managers
2123	Agricultural Representatives, Consultants and Specialists
2271	Air Pilots, Flight Engineers and Flying Instructors
2272	Air Traffic Control and Related Occupations
2244	Aircraft Instrument, Electrical and Avionics Mechanics, Technicians and Inspectors
7315	Aircraft Mechanics and Aircraft Inspectors
3234	Ambulance Attendants and Other Paramedical Occupations
5231	Announcers and Other Broadcasters
8257	Aquaculture Operators and Managers
2151	Architects
2251	Architectural Technologists and Technicians
0212	Architecture and Science Managers
5113	Archivists
5244	Artisans and Craftpersons
1235	Assessors, Valuators and Appraisers
5251	Athletes
5225	Audio and Video Recording Technicians
3141	Audiologists and Speech-Language Pathologists

[1]For more information about the NOC, see Chapter 2.

2224	Conservation and Fishery Officers
5112	Conservators and Curators
2234	Construction Estimators
2264	Construction Inspectors
0711	Construction Managers
7311	Construction Millwrights and Industrial Mechanics (Except Textile)
7215	Contractors and Supervisors, Carpentry Trades
7212	Contractors and Supervisors, Electrical Trades and Telecommunications
7217	Contractors and Supervisors, Heavy Construction Equipment Crews
7216	Contractors and Supervisors, Mechanic Trades
7214	Contractors and Supervisors, Metal Forming, Shaping and Erecting Trades
7219	Contractors and Supervisors, Other Construction Trades, Installers, Repairers
7213	Contractors and Supervisors, Pipefitting Trades
6242	Cooks
1227	Court Officers and Justices of the Peace
1244	Court Recorders and Medical Transcriptionists
7371	Crane Operators
1236	Customs, Ship and Other Brokers

D

5134	Dancers
2172	Database Analysts and Data Administrators
2273	Deck Officers, Water Transport
3222	Dental Hygienists and Dental Therapists
3223	Dental Technologists, Technicians and Laboratory
3113	Dentists
3221	Denturists
3132	Dietitians and Nutritionists
2253	Drafting Technologists and Technicians
7372	Drillers and Blasters D Surface Mining, Quarrying and Construction
6214	Dry Cleaning and Laundry Supervisors

E

4214	Early Childhood Educators and Assistants
4162	Economists and Economic Policy Researchers and Analysts
5122	Editors
4166	Education Policy Researchers, Consultants and Program Officers
4143	Educational Counsellors
7332	Electric Appliance Servicers and Repairers

2241	Electrical and Electronics Engineering Technologists and Technicians
2133	Electrical and Electronics Engineers
7333	Electrical Mechanics
7244	Electrical Power Line and Cable Workers
7241	Electricians (Except Industrial and Power System)
3218	Electroencephalographic and Other Diagnostic Technologists, n.e.c.
2242	Electronic Service Technicians (Household and Business
7318	Elevator Constructors and Mechanics
4213	Employment Counsellors
2274	Engineer Officers, Water Transport
2262	Engineering Inspectors and Regulatory Officers
0211	Engineering Managers
1222	Executive Assistants
6213	Executive Housekeepers

F

0721	Facility Operation and Maintenance Managers
4153	Family, Marriage and Other Related Counsellors
8253	Farm Supervisors and Specialized Livestock Workers
8251	Farmers and Farm Managers
5222	Film and Video Camera Operators
1112	Financial and Investment Analysts
1111	Financial Auditors and Accountants
0111	Financial Managers
1114	Financial Officers (other)
0642	Fire Chiefs and Senior Firefighting Officers
6262	Firefighters
8261	Fishing Masters and Officers
8262	Fishing Vessel Skippers and Fishermen/women
7295	Floor Covering Installers
6212	Food Service Supervisors
2122	Forestry Professionals
2223	Forestry Technologists and Technicians
6272	Funeral Directors and Embalmers

G

7253	Gas Fitters
2212	Geological and Mineral Technologists and Technicians
2144	Geological Engineers
2113	Geologists, Geochemists and Geophysicists
7292	Glaziers
0412	Government Managers – Economic Analysis, Policy Development
0413	Government Managers – Education Policy Development and Program Administration

N

4161	Natural and Applied Science Policy Researchers, Consultants and Program Officers
2261	Nondestructive Testers and Inspectors
8254	Nursery and Greenhouse Operators and Managers

O

3143	Occupational Therapists
8232	Oil and Gas Well Drillers, Servicers, Testers and Related Workers
7331	Oil and Solid Fuel Heating Mechanics
3231	Opticians
3121	Optometrists

P

7294	Painters and Decorators
5136	Painters, Sculptors and Other Visual Artists
9234	Papermaking and Coating Control Operators
4211	Paralegal and Related Occupations
5245	Patternmakers – Textile, Leather and Fur Products
5232	Performers (other)
1223	Personnel and Recruitment Officers
2145	Petroleum Engineers
9232	Petroleum, Gas and Chemical Process Operators
3131	Pharmacists
5221	Photographers
2115	Physical Sciences (Other Professional Occupations)
3112	Physicians – General Practitioners and Family Physicians
3111	Physicians – Specialist
2111	Physicists and Astronomers
3142	Physiotherapists
7252	Pipefitters
7284	Plasterers, Drywall Installers and Finishers and Lathers
7251	Plumbers
6261	Police Officers (Except Commissioned)
0132	Postal and Courier Services Managers
4122	Post-Secondary Teaching and Research Assistants
7243	Power System Electricians
7352	Power Systems and Power Station Operators
0811	Primary Production Managers (Except Agriculture)
7381	Printing Press Operators
4155	Probation and Parole Officers and Related Occupations
5131	Producers, Directors, Choreographers and Related Occupations
2148	Professional Engineers, n.e.c. (other)
1122	Professional Occupations in Business Services to Management

5124   Professional Occupations in Public
        Relations and Communications
4121   Professors – University
5254   Program Leaders and Instructors in Recreation and Sport
4168   Program Officers Unique to Government
1224   Property Administrators
4151   Psychologists
9233   Pulping Control Operators
1225   Purchasing Agents and Officers
0113   Purchasing Managers

R
7361   Railway and Yard Locomotive Engineers
7314   Railway Carmen/women
7362   Railway Conductors and Brakemen/women
2275   Railway Traffic Controllers and Marine Traffic Regulators
6232   Real Estate Agents and Salespersons
0513   Recreation and Sports Program and Service Directors
4167   Recreation, Sports and Fitness Program Supervisors
        Consultants
7313   Refrigeration and Air Conditioning Mechanics
3152   Registered Nurses
4217   Religious Occupations (other)
0712   Residential Home Builders and Renovators
3214   Respiratory Therapists, Clinical Perfusionists and
        Cardio-Pulmonary Technologists
0631   Restaurant and Food Service Managers
6233   Retail and Wholesale Buyers
0621   Retail Trade Managers
6211   Retail Trade Supervisors
7291   Roofers and Shinglers

S
0611   Sales, Marketing and Advertising Managers
0313   School Principals and Administrators of Elementary and
        Secondary
1241   Secretaries (Except Legal and Medical)
1113   Securities Agents, Investment Dealers and Brokers
0012   Senior Government Managers and Officials
0013   Senior Managers – Financial, Communications and Other
        Business
0016   Senior Managers – Goods Production, Utilities,
        Transportation and Construction
0014   Senior Managers – Health, Education, Social and Community
0015   Senior Managers – Trade, Broadcasting and Other
        Services, n.e.c.
6216   Service Supervisors (other)
0651   Services Managers (other)

7261	Sheet Metal Workers
7343	Shoe Repairers and Shoemakers
7335	Small Engine and Equipment Mechanics (other)
4164	Social Policy Researchers, Consultants and Program Officers
4169	Social Science, n.e.c. (Other Professional Occupations)
4152	Social Workers
2173	Software Engineers
1121	Specialists in Human Resources
5253	Sports Officials and Referees
7252	Sprinkler System Installers
7351	Stationary Engineers and Auxiliary Equipment Operators
7252	Steamfitters, Pipefitters and Sprinkler System Installers
7263	Structural Metal and Platework Fabricators and Fitters
9223	Supervisors, Electrical Products Manufacturing
9222	Supervisors, Electronics Manufacturing
9225	Supervisors, Fabric, Fur and Leather Products Manufacturing
1212	Supervisors, Finance and Insurance Clerks
9213	Supervisors, Food, Beverage and Tobacco Processing
9215	Supervisors, Forest Products Processing
9224	Supervisors, Furniture and Fixtures Manufacturing
1211	Supervisors, General Office and Administrative Support Clerks
8256	Supervisors, Landscape and Horticulture
1213	Supervisors, Library, Correspondence and Related Information Clerks
8211	Supervisors, Logging and Forestry
7211	Supervisors, Machinists and Related Occupations
1214	Supervisors, Mail and Message Distribution Occupations
9211	Supervisors, Mineral and Metal Processing
8221	Supervisors, Mining and Quarrying
7222	Supervisors, Motor Transport and Other Ground Transit Operators
9221	Supervisors, Motor Vehicle Assembling
8222	Supervisors, Oil and Gas Drilling and Service
9226	Supervisors, Other Mechanical and Metal Products Manufacturing
9227	Supervisors, Other Products Manufacturing and Assembly
9212	Supervisors, Petroleum, Gas and Chemical Processing and Utilities
9214	Supervisors, Plastic and Rubber Products Manufacturing
7218	Supervisors, Printing and Related Occupations
7221	Supervisors, Railway Transport Operations
1215	Supervisors, Recording, Distributing and Scheduling Occupations
9216	Supervisors, Textile Processing

SCHEDULE 6
INFORMATION REGARDING LANGUAGE TESTS

English language testing organisations

French language testing organisations

The University of Cambridge Local Examination Syndicate, Education Australia, and the British Council administer the International English Language Testing System (**IELTS**).
Note: IELTS has 'General Training' and 'Academic' options for the reading and writing tests. If you choose to take an IELTS test, you must take the 'General Training' option.

The University of British Columbia's Applied Research and Evaluation Services (ARES) administer the Canadian International Language Proficiency Index Program (**CELPIP**).

The Paris Chamber of Commerce and Industry administers the Test d'Évaluation de Français (**TEF**).
Note: For immigration purposes, you must submit results for the following tests:
– expression orale,
– compréhension orale,
– compréhension écrite,
– expression écrite.

To find out more details about these tests and about taking them, visit the following web sites:

◆ International English Language Testing System (**IELTS**) **www.ielts.org/**

◆ Canadian International Language Proficiency Index Program (**CELPIP**) **www.lpi.ubc.ca/CELPIP/index.html**

◆ Test d'Évaluation de Français (**TEF**) **www.fda.ccip.fr/sinformer/tef/**

SCHEDULE 7
WEB SITES OF CANADIAN VISA OFFICES ABROAD[1]

Asia and Pacific
Sydney, Australia **www.dfait-maeci.gc.ca/australia**

Dhaka, Bangladesh **www.chcdhaka**

China – Beijing, Shanghai **www.canada.org.cn**

Hong Kong, China **www.dfait-maeci.gc.ca/hongkong**

New Delhi, India **www.dfait-maeci.gc.ca/new-delhi**

Jakarta, Indonesia **www.dfait-maeci.gc.ca/jakarta**

Tokyo, Japan **www.canadanet.or.jp**

Seoul, South Korea **www.korea.gc.ca**

Kuala Lumpur, Malaysia **www.dfait-maeci.gc.ca/
   kualalumpur**

Islamabad, Pakistan **www.dfait-maeci.gc.ca/islamabad**

Manila, Philippines **www.dfait-maeci.gc.ca/manila**

Singapore, Singapore **www.dfait-maeci.gc.ca/singapore**

Colombo, Sri Lanka N/A

Taipei, Taiwan **www.canada.org.tw**

Bangkok, Thailand **www.dfait-maeci.gc.ca/bangkok**

Ho Chi Minh City, Vietnam **www.dfait-maeci.gc.ca/vietnam**

Europe
Vienna, Austria **www.kanada.at**

Prague, Czech Republic **www.canada.cz**

Paris, France **www.dfait-maeci.gc.ca/canadaeuropa/france/**

Berlin, Germany **www.dfait-maeci.gc.ca/canadaeuropa/
   germany/**

[1]For updated information on this topic and contact information for visa offices without web sites, please visit **www.cic.gc.ca**. Please note that Canadian missions that do not process permanent or temporary residence applications are not listed here.

Budapest, Hungary **www.dfait-maeci.gc.ca/budapest**
Rome, Italy **www.dfait-maeci.gc.ca/canadaeuropa/italy/**
Warsaw, Poland **www.canada.pl**
Bucharest, Romania **www.dfait-maeci.gc.ca/bucharest**
Moscow, Russia **www.canadaeuropa.gc.ca/russia**
St Petersburg, Russia N/A
Belgrade, Serbia-Montenegro **www.canada.org.yu**
Ankara, Turkey **www.dfait-maeci.gc.ca/ankara**
Kyiv, Ukraine **www.canadaeuropa.gc.ca/ukraine/**
London, United Kingdom **www.canada.org.uk**

Africa and Middle East
Yaounde, Cameroon N/A
Cairo, Egypt **www.dfait-maeci.gc.ca/cairo/**
Accra, Ghana **www.dfait-maeci.gc.ca/accra**
Conakry, Guinea N/A
Tehran, Iran N/A
Tel Aviv, Israel **www.dfait-maeci.gc.ca/telaviv**
Abidjan, Ivory Coast **www.dfait-maeci.gc.ca/abidjan/**
Amman, Jordan N/A
Nairobi, Kenya N/A
Kuwait City, Kuwait **www.dfait-maeci.gc.ca/kuwait**
Beirut, Lebanon **www.dfait-maeci.gc.ca/beirut**
Rabat, Morocco N/A
Lagos, Nigeria N/A
Riyadh, Saudi Arabia N/A
Dakar, Senegal **www.dfait-maeci.gc.ca/dakar**
Pretoria, South Africa **www.dfait-maeci.gc.ca/southafrica/**
Damascus, Syria **www.dfait-maeci.gc.ca/syria**
Tunis, Tunisia **www.dfait-maeci.gc.ca/tunisia**
Abu Dhabi, United Arab Emirates
   www.dfait-maeci.gc.ca/abudhabi

Lusaka, Zambia N/A
Harare, Zimbabwe N/A

Western hemisphere

Buenos Aires, Argentina **www.dfait-maeci.gc.ca/bairs**
São Paulo, Brazil **www.dfait-maeci.gc.ca/brazil/**
Santiago, Chile **www.dfait-maeci.gc.ca/chile/**
Bogota, Colombia **www.dfait-maeci.gc.ca/colombia**
Havana, Cuba N/A
Santo Domingo, Dominican Republic
    www.dfait-maeci.gc.ca/dominicanrepublic/
Quito, Ecuador N/A
San Salvador, El Salvador **www.dfait-maeci.gc.ca/elsalvador**
Guatemala City, Guatemala N/A
Port-au-Prince, Haiti **www.dfait-maeci.gc.ca/haiti/**
Kingston, Jamaica **www.dfait-maeci.gc.ca/jamaica/**
Mexico City, Mexico **www.dfait-maeci.gc.ca/mexico-city/**
Lima, Peru **www.dfait-maeci.gc.ca/peru/**
Port of Spain, Trinidad and Tobago
    www.dfait-maeci.gc.ca/trinidadtobago
Buffalo, U.S.A. **www.dfait-maeci.gc.ca/buffalo**
Detroit, U.S.A. **www.dfait-maeci.gc.ca/detroit**
Los Angeles, U.S.A. **www.dfait-maeci.gc.ca/los_angeles**
New York, U.S.A. **www.dfait-maeci.gc.ca/new_york**
Seattle, U.S.A. **www.dfait-maeci.gc.ca/seattle**
Washington, U.S.A. **www.can-am.gc.ca/washington**
Caracas, Venezuela **www.dfait-maeci.gc.ca/caracas**

SCHEDULE 8
CONTACTING CIC INSIDE CANADA

If you are in the local calling area of:	Phone number:
Montreal	(514) 496-1010
Toronto	(416) 973-4444
Vancouver	(604) 666-2171
Anywhere else in Canada	1-888-242-2100
	Toll free number

SCHEDULE 9

▮✦▮ Citizenship and Immigration Canada	Citoyenneté et Immigration Canada	PAGE 1 OF 3 PROTECTED WHEN COMPLETED - B

APPLICATION TO CHANGE CONDITIONS OR TO EXTEND MY STAY IN CANADA

NOTE: This form can be used to request/apply for more than one of the below for yourself or your family members. Payment of fees does not guarantee approval of the application.

I AM APPLYING FOR: ▶ "A" ☐ Extension of Temporary Resident Status as a Visitor "B" ☐ Initial Study Permit or Renewal "C" ☐ Initial Work Permit or Renewal "D" ☐ Temporary Resident Permit "E" ☐ Restoration of Temporary Resident Status

I want service in ☐ English ☐ French

Client ID Number

A - PERSONAL INFORMATION

1 Surname (Family name) | Given name(s)

Other name(s) used | Sex ☐ Male ☐ Female

Date of birth D M Y | Place of birth (City, state/province and country)

Citizenship | Passport number | Date of issue D M Y | Expiry date D M Y | Country of last permanent residence | ☐ Since birth ☐ Since the year

MARITAL STATUS ▶ ☐ Never married ☐ Married ▶ If you are married, is your spouse a Canadian citizen or permanent resident? ☐ Yes ☐ No | ☐ Widowed ☐ Separated ☐ Divorced ☐ Common-law partner

My residential address in Canada | My current mailing address in Canada (if different from my residential address). All correspondence will go to this address. If you wish to authorize the release of information from your case file to a representative, indicate their address below and on the form IMM 5476

No. and street | Apt./Unit | No. and street | Apt./Unit

City/Town | Province | Postal code | City/Town | Province | Postal code

Telephone number in Canada: Area code | Fax number: Area code | Telephone number in Canada for messages: Area code

B - MY FAMILY MEMBERS

2 Surname (Family name) | Given name(s) | Relationship | Client ID number

Date of birth D M Y | Country of birth | Country of last permanent residence | Citizenship

Passport number | Date of issue D M Y | Expiry date D M Y | Type(s) of document requested ☐ A ☐ B ☐ C ☐ D ☐ E ☐ None

My family member is in Canada? ☐ Yes ☐ No

3 Surname (Family name) | Given name(s) | Relationship | Client ID number

Date of birth D M Y | Country of birth | Country of last permanent residence | Citizenship

Passport number | Date of issue D M Y | Expiry date D M Y | Type(s) of document requested ☐ A ☐ B ☐ C ☐ D ☐ E ☐ None

My family member is in Canada? ☐ Yes ☐ No

4 Surname (Family name) | Given name(s) | Relationship | Client ID number

Date of birth D M Y | Country of birth | Country of last permanent residence | Citizenship

Passport number | Date of issue D M Y | Expiry date D M Y | Type(s) of document requested ☐ A ☐ B ☐ C ☐ D ☐ E ☐ None

My family member is in Canada? ☐ Yes ☐ No

IMM 1249 (08-2002) E | (DISPONIBLE EN FRANÇAIS - IMM 1249 F) | Canada

5 Surname (Family name)	Given name(s)	Relationship	Client ID number

Date of birth	D M Y	Country of birth	Country of last permanent residence	Citizenship

Passport number	Date of issue D M Y	Expiry date D M Y	Type(s) of document requested □ A □ B □ C □ D □ E □ None

My family member is in Canada? □ Yes □ No

6 Surname (Family name)	Given name(s)	Relationship	Client ID number

Date of birth	D M Y	Country of birth	Country of last permanent residence	Citizenship

Passport number	Date of issue D M Y	Expiry date D M Y	Type(s) of document requested □ A □ B □ C □ D □ E □ None

My family member is in Canada? □ Yes □ No

C - COMING INTO CANADA

7 Original entry to Canada	Date D M Y	8 Most recent entry to Canada (if not the same as original entry)	Date D M Y
Place (city, province)		Place (city, province)	

9 My original reason for coming to Canada

D - MY REQUEST

10 I want to: ▶ □ extend my stay in Canada until   D M Y   □ extend the stay of my family members in Canada until   D M Y   AND / OR □ change conditions

for the following reasons (Give complete details)

11 To support myself in Canada

I have $ _____ (Canadian dollars) available.

I receive support from: □ Self □ Relative □ Friend □ General Welfare Assistance □ Other

Other details

IMM 1249 (08-2002) E

E - ADDITIONAL INFORMATION

12 If you or your family members

- remained beyond the validity of your status
- attended school without authorization
- worked without authorization

please give the reasons and circumstances concerning the situation(s)

13 Have you or any of your family members in Canada ever been convicted of or charged with a crime or offence in any country?

If "yes", give details (name, date and place of charge; name, date and place of conviction, offence, sentence).
If you require more space, use a separate sheet of paper.

☐ YES ☐ NO

14 Have you or any of your family members in Canada suffered from any serious mental or physical illness?

If "yes", give details (name of illness, period of illness, treatment received). If you require more space, use a separate sheet of paper.

☐ YES ☐ NO

F - PHOTOGRAPHS - REQUIRED ONLY IF YOU ARE APPLYING FOR EXTENSION OF YOUR TEMPORARY RESIDENT PERMIT

Staple two (2) recent passport-size photographs of yourself and each family member in Canada to the top of the front page of the aplication (do not use glue). Print the name and date of birth of the person on the back of each photograph.

G - DECLARATION OF APPLICANT

IMPORTANT: YOU MUST READ AND SIGN THIS SECTION

I declare that the information I have given in this application is truthful, complete and correct. I understand that any statement or concealment of a material fact may result in my removal from Canada.

	Day	Month	Year

_____
Signature of applicant

Date

SCHEDULE 10
GATS MEMBER COUNTRIES

Algeria	Grenada	Norway
Angola	Greece	Pakistan
Antigua and Barbuda	Guatemala	Paraguay
Argentina	Guinea-Bissau	Peru
Australia	Guyana	Philippines
Austria	Haiti	Poland
Bahrain	Honduras	Portugal
Bangladesh	Hong Kong	Qatar
Barbados	Hungary	Romania
Belgium	Iceland	Rwanda
Belize	India	Saint Lucia
Benin	Indonesia	St Kitts and Nevis
Bolivia	Ireland	St Vincent and the Grenadines
Botswana	Israel	Senegal
Brazil	Italy	Sierra Leone
Brunei	Jamaica	Singapore
Burkina Faso	Japan	Slovak Republic
Burundi	Kenya	Slovenia
Cameroon	Korea, Rep. of	South Africa
Canada	Kuwait	Spain
Central African	Republic Lesotho	Sri Lanka
Chad	Liechtenstein	Surinam
Chile	Luxembourg	Swaziland
Colombia	Macau	Sweden
Congo	Madagascar	Switzerland
Costa	Rica Malawi	Tanzania
Cote d'Ivoire	Malaysia	Thailand
Cuba	Maldives	Togo
Cyprus	Mali	Trinidad and Tobago
Czech Republic	Malta	Tunisia
Denmark	Mauritania	Turkey
Dominica	Mauritius	Uganda
Dominican Republic	Mexico	United Arab Emirates
Egypt	Morocco	United Kingdom
El Salvador	Mozambique	Uruguay
Fiji	Myanmar	United States of America
Finland	Namibia	Venezuela
France	Netherlands	Zaire
Gabon	New Zealand	Zambia
Gambia	Nicaragua	Zimbabwe
Germany	Niger	
Ghana	Nigeria	

SCHEDULE 11
LINKS TO EMPLOYMENT AGENCIES

Recruiters Online Network **www.recruitersonline.com/**

Jenex Technology Placement Inc. **www.jenex.ca/**

Eagle Professional Resources Inc. **www.eagleonline.com/**

The Design Group **www.eagleonline.com/**

Corporate Recruiters Ltd.

   www.corporate.bc.ca/cfm/index.cfm

Advanced Technology Partners **www.atpstaff.com/**

Glossary

Citizenship and Immigration Canada (CIC) The department in charge of immigration matters.

Common-law partner A person of the same or opposite sex who has lived with you in a conjugal relationship for a period of at least one year.

Confirmation of Permanent Residence (COPR) A form that the relevant visa office will issue to you. It contains all of your identification information, as well as a photo and your signature.

Dependent children Daughters and sons, of the principal applicant or his or her spouse, including children adopted before the age of 18, who:

- are under the age of 22 and do not have a spouse or common-law partner; or
- have been continuously enrolled and in attendance as full-time students in an educational institution and financially supported by their parents since turning 22 (or from the date of becoming a spouse or common-law partner if this happened before the age of 22); or
- have substantially depended on the financial support of their parents since before turning 22 and are unable to support themselves due to a medical condition.

Educational credential Any diploma, degree, trade or apprenticeship credential issued for the completion of a programme of study or training at a recognised educational or training institution.

Family member A spouse, common-law partner or dependent child, or dependent child of a dependent child of the principal applicant. The spouse or common-law partner of the principal applicant's dependent child is also considered a family member.

Human Resources and Skills Development Canada (HRSDC) The department in charge of employment development in Canada. Their input is often necessary in work permit applications, and for arranged employment.

National Occupational Classification (NOC) A list containing the classification system of occupations in Canada. It describes the duties, skills, aptitudes and work settings typical of jobs in the Canadian labour market. See Chapter 2 for more details.

Nomination Certificate (NC) A certificate issued in the context of provincial nomination. See Chapter 5 for more details.

Not applicable (N/A) See Chapter 1, section 1:2.3.a for more information on the use of N/A.

Permanent employment Employment for an indefinite amount of time.

Permanent Residence Card A document which allows you to travel to Canada on commercial carriers, and in many cases will be seen as de facto proof of residency in Canada. It will be sent to you after your arrival in Canada.

Post-secondary education Education undertaken after completion of high-school education.

Provincial Nominee Program(s) (PNP) Immigration programmes that are established under agreements between the Federal Government of Canada and individual provinces. They are covered in more detail in Chapter 5.

Relevant visa office The visa office where you should submit your application. See Chapter 1, section 1:2.1, for details on how to find out what is the relevant visa office in your case.

Secondary education High-school education.

Skilled workers People who may become permanent residents based on their ability to become economically established in Canada.

Spouse A person of the opposite sex who is 16 years of age or older and to whom the principal applicant is legally married.

Temporary employment Employment for a limited period of time. An offer for such employment is made in the context of a work permit application. See Chapter 7 for more details on work permits/temporary employment.

Temporary resident A person who has been admitted in Canada for a limited period of time. Students, foreign workers and visitors are examples of temporary residents.

Temporary Resident Visa (TRV) A document issued and placed in your passport by a visa office abroad. It shows that you have met the requirements for admission in Canada as a temporary resident. See Chapter 9 for more information.

Visa office/Visa post An Embassy, High Commission or consulate handling immigration matters is often referred to as a visa office or visa post.

Work An activity for which wages or commission is earned, or that competes directly with activities of Canadian citizens or permanent residents in the Canadian labour market.

Work permit A written authorisation to work in Canada issued to a person who is not a Canadian citizen or a permanent resident of Canada. It is required whether or not the employer is in Canada. Usually it is valid only for a specified job and length of time. See Chapter 7 for more information.

Index